RISE AND SHINE

RISE AND

SHINE

LIZ CURTIS HIGGS

WATERBROOK
PRESS

RISE AND SHINE
PUBLISHED BY WATERBROOK PRESS
2375 Telstar Drive, Suite 160
Colorado Springs, Colorado 80920
A division of Random House, Inc.

Material previously published in *"While Shepherds Washed Their Flocks" and Other Funny Things Kids Say and Do* (1998), *Help! I'm Laughing and I Can't Get Up* (1998), *Mirror, Mirror on the Wall, Have I Got News for You!* (1997), *Forty Reasons Why Life Is More Fun After the Big 40* (1997), *Reflecting His Image* (1996), *Only Angels Can Wing It, the Rest of Us Have to Practice* (1995), *"One Size Fits All" and Other Fables* (1993), *Does Dinner in a Bucket Count?* (1993). Portions previously appeared in *Today's Christian Woman*, a publication of CTI, Inc.

ISBN 1-4000-7000-7

Rise and Shine was originally published by Thomas Nelson in 2002.

Library of Congress Cataloging-in-Publication Data
Higgs, Liz Curtis.
    Rise and shine / Liz Curtis Higgs.—1st WaterBrook Press ed.
        p. cm.
    Originally published: Nashville : T. Nelson Publishers, c2002.
    Includes bibliographical references.
    ISBN 1-4000-7000-7
    1. Devotional literature, English. I. Title.
    BV4832.3.H54 2004
    242—dc22
                            2004013743

Printed in the United States of America
2004

10 9 8 7 6 5 4 3

Contents

Rise and Shine, Sister Mine

Arise, shine;
For your light has come!
And the glory of the LORD is risen upon you.

—*Isaiah 60:1*

When you **rise** from your bed, rubbing the sleep out of your eyes and the tangles out of your disheveled hair, how many minutes does it take before you can truly **shine**?

Oh, dear. That long.

Might I have just *two* of those precious minutes each morning?

Two minutes to whisper a gentle word of encouragement, to brush a feather across your funny bone, to prove how beautiful and valuable you are to God.

Say yes, sis.

The most important part will be our first few seconds together, as you drink in the living water of God's Word. My own simple words will follow, closing with a prayer from my heart to yours. Only two or three pages, then you can put *Rise and Shine* aside and reach for your morning coffee.

Like the varied images on the cover of this book, the tone and subject of each day's message will be quite different—some are playful, some inspiring, others more serious. Promise me you'll only read one chapter a day, or you might suffer from spiritual whiplash!

You'll find occasional references to surveys or quotes from, say, "Nancy from New York." For years I gathered information and stories from readers, and so they're quoted here. Just think of them as friends you haven't met yet.

If you've already read several of my early nonfiction titles, from *Does Dinner in a Bucket Count?* to *"While Shepherds Washed Their Flocks" and Other Funny Things Kids Say and Do,* or some of my articles in *Today's Christian Woman,* then—bless your generous, supportive heart!—this may not be all-new material for you. But if you and I have met only recently across the printed page, then *Rise and Shine* will be the perfect way for us to catch up with one another.

Perhaps you are doing more than rising from the comfort of your bed. You may be rising from the depths of a disastrous lifestyle or a painful relationship, determined to start fresh. Arise, beloved sister. Strong hands await to hold you steady.

Perhaps you fear you've lost your shine. The glow of good health, the sparkle of young love, the shimmer of a new mother's tears—all have faded into a gray sort of daily grind. Fear not. Turn with me toward the radiant One and let his light be reflected in your countenance like the dawn of a summer day.

Two minutes. No calories, no squat thrusts, I promise.

Rise, sister mine. And shine.

Lord, what an honor it will be to start the day with you.
Give me the strength to lift my head,
the courage to lift my heart,
the joy to lift my spirits,
and the confidence to lift my eyes and see you
rising and shining in me.

MIRROR IMAGE

He has made everything beautiful in its time.

—*ECCLESIASTES 3:11*

Looked in the mirror yet this morning, babe? And did you like what you saw?

Most of us see double chins, tiny wrinkles, ugly blemishes, spreading crow's-feet, dark circles under our eyes—the list goes on and on.

Truth is, we seldom look in a mirror unless we're looking for a problem.

"Does my hair look okay?"

"Do I need more lipstick?"

"Is my slip showing?"

And the classic: "Does this dress make me look fat?"

What if this morning you saw a woman who is uniquely created by God in his image? A woman who isn't "better than" or "worse than" or in need of an overhaul. And one who is definitely happy! Because trust me, that's what I see.

When I look at you, dear one, sitting out there in the third row at one of my presentations, when I see your upturned face, full of life, ready to laugh, I do not see wrinkles, blemishes, or double chins. I do not see figure flaws or flabby thighs. I see a beautiful woman. One who is radiantly alive, willing to learn, ready to grow, expectant, joy-filled, eager to embrace all that life has to offer.

You are something else!

That's not me, you may say. *I'm not in your third row. I'm here at home, and I'm miserable, and I hate my lumpy body, and radiant is not what I feel.*

Understood.

What I'm talking about transcends feelings and moves into the realm of faith in order to become fact. That radiant, alive woman is in you, even if you can't see her yet. She was hiding in me for decades before I realized it, and she is in you now. And she wants *out!*

The Lord created and defined beauty in our world. Surely he didn't make lovely butterflies, exquisite flowers, and gorgeous sunsets and leave out womankind, the crown of his creation? Not likely!

When we stop listening to what Madison Avenue and Hollywood tell us is beautiful and start listening to our hearts and God's Word, they will not steer us wrong. Even though we may never look like ultrathin models or movie stars, those famous women (poor things) will never get to look like *us!*

By God's design, women come in all shapes and sizes—large and small, short and tall. In every home, in every workplace, in every social setting, in every church, there are as many different sizes, shapes, colors, and characteristics as there are women.

Luci Swindoll says, "When you love yourself and accept yourself for who you are, you have nothing left to prove."[1] So right. Each one of us is different, beloved. And those differences are good.

Lord Jesus, help me see myself as you do:
beautifully made according to your divine design.
Forgive me for comparing myself to others and wishing I were different.
Starting today, let me not only accept my own appearance
but also accept others exactly as they are,
knowing that they, too, were created in your image.

Good Groom-ing

And as the bridegroom rejoices over the bride,
So shall your God rejoice over you.

—Isaiah 62:5b

Flying home from Atlanta one Saturday evening, I sat next to a young woman who was impeccably groomed in every way, except for the streaks on her cheeks where tears had washed away some of her rosy red blush.

My heart went out to her, but my head said, *None of your business, Liz. Don't interfere.*

As usual, I ignored my head and went with my heart. "What brings you to Louisville?" I asked softly.

She turned my direction, and a fresh flow of tears began. "I don't know!"

Inside, a still, small voice got my attention: *Hush, Liz! Let her talk.* I pressed my lips together (for me, that's almost an aerobic exercise), assumed my most compassionate expression, and simply nodded.

"I'm g-g-getting married," she stammered, daintily blowing her perfectly powdered nose.

"How wonderful!" I exclaimed, my vow of silence forgotten.

"I'm not so sure." Her voice was high and strained. "My entire family and all my friends live in Florida, plus I have a great job there. I'm leaving my whole life behind." Another trickle of tears slipped out of the corner of her eye.

"I moved to Louisville from far away too," I explained, trying to comfort her. "It's a great place to live."

"I guess so," she murmured, sounding unconvinced.

Despite my efforts, I was not helping one bit. Until the perfect question suddenly presented itself. "Do you love him?"

Her expression changed instantly. "Oh, yes!" She blushed at her own enthusiasm, then stumbled over a rush of words. "He's very kind and considerate, really intelligent, and handsome too." As she brushed away the last of her tears, she told me about her beloved husband-to-be—how much fun they had together, how impressed her family was with him, and, yes, how much she loved him.

I nodded and listened, knowing no further questions would be needed.

When we landed and headed into the gate area, I picked him out of the crowd instantly. Even from a distance, he was obviously a fine young man. Tall and broad-shouldered, he was armed with a warm, welcoming grin and a dozen red roses that matched her red suit perfectly. When she ran into his embrace with a teary smile, I made myself look away (very difficult!) rather than invade their privacy. A few happy tears sneaked into my own eyes.

When you find the right One, it's easy to forsake all others and follow him.

Lord, you are the best husband a woman could hope for.
Help me release my earthly cares and cleave to you,
knowing that your love is certain and your provision
is sufficient for all my needs.
No one loves me more than you do, Jesus.
And your love is enough.

Guilt, Guilt, Go Away

*. . . casting all your care upon Him,
for He cares for you.*

—1 PETER 5:7

My audiences often ask me if I miss my children when I'm on the road speaking. Absolutely. (Although it *is* nice to look out on a room full of people who dressed themselves.)

For moms who travel, airport card shops now feature colorful greeting cards to mail to your kids back home. They have warm thoughts inside like, "Can't wait to hug you again" or "Mama misses you s-o-o-o-o much." What they really mean is, "Help! I'm on a guilt trip."

If you ask women what they want more of in their lives, they never shout out, "Sex!" or "Money!" Their response is always the same: "Time!" (I know, I know—if you had more time, you also might have more of the other two.) A working mother in Lansing wrote, "There just isn't enough of me to go around." Yeah, we get that.

No matter what our station in life, there is a guilt message formulated just for us. Single women hear: "Why don't you get out more? You'll never meet someone sitting at home." Married women hear: "So when are you going to start a family?" Mothers at home hear: "What do you do all day?" Working mothers hear: "But who cares for your children while you work?"

Ayeeee!

Some of us have an internal "guilt table" to determine how badly we should feel:

Falling asleep during the 6:00 P.M. news *2*
Sending store-bought cookies to school. *5*
Forgetting to pick up child (first time). *9*
Forgetting to pick up child (second time) *342*

If too many tasks and not enough time sounds like life at your house, the solution is as close as Sesame Street. Just practice saying those two little letters in the middle of the alphabet: *N* and *O!*

Teach me to say NO, Lord.
NO to too many activities.
NO to too much time apart from my family.
And NO to self-imposed guilt.
I welcome the conviction of your
Holy Spirit, Lord.
I long for your wisdom
and discernment, always.
But when it comes to guilt . . .
NO, thanks.

Beautiful to Behold

*For the L*ORD* takes pleasure in His people;*
He will beautify the humble with salvation.

—P*SALM 149:4*

When women kindly ask me to sign their copies of my books, I sometimes write, "To Susan the Beautiful!"

. "Oh, no!" Susan (or Kathy or Linda) will protest, turning red. "I'm not beautiful."

"Sure you are," I insist, as I add my signature. "It says so right in the Bible." As further proof, I jot down "Psalm 149:4" and encourage them to look it up. You see, it's God's gift of salvation that makes us truly beautiful, inside and out. Nothing transforms a woman's appearance more than being covered from head to toe in the grace of God's Son.

I know this beautifying process is legitimate because I've seen it happen again and again. When women come to know the Lord in a real and personal way, their frown lines begin to soften. A sparkle appears in their eyes, and a radiance falls over their countenance.

We have proven scientifically that such physical changes occur when we fall in love: glowing skin, sparkling eyes, increased heart rate. And for some of us, similar improvements take place when we're expecting a child. Conventional wisdom says that "all brides are beautiful" and "pregnant women glow." It's chemical, hormonal, and very real.

Why not at the spiritual level too? When you allow the Lord to fill your heart with his boundless love, it shows on the outside. This beauty has nothing to do with cosmetics or plastic surgery. On the contrary, it's an inside job: A heart full of love produces a face full of joy.

When I stepped into a church for the first time as an adult, I was amazed to see pew after pew of attractive women. *Is this a requirement of membership?* I wondered. *Maybe they're all Mary Kay consultants . . .*

Soon I learned the happy truth: Such beauty is a gift from God. Unlike lipstick and blush, which seldom last longer than a few hours, spiritual beauty is timeless. It literally pours out of your pores and alters your appearance in a most appealing way. People will think you've had a face-lift, when in fact you've had a *faith*-lift!

Lord, as I sit at my makeup mirror this morning,
help me see the subtle yet significant ways you are turning me
into your kind of beautiful woman.
Shine through my eyes, Jesus. Pour out my pores.
Let your joy lift my lips into a hundred-watt smile.

Door-to-Door Service

The LORD is my rock and my fortress and my deliverer;
The God of my strength, in whom I will trust.

—2 SAMUEL 22:2B–3A

Have you always trusted God, my friend?

Or did you, like me, come to know him a bit farther down life's road?

Despite my parents' best efforts to raise a wholesome, small-town girl, I veered off track in my teens and started hanging out with a faster crowd. First it was sneaking a cigarette out of Mom's purse. Then it was cutting school for an hour, then an afternoon, then a whole day. I smoked my first joint on our senior class trip. Most of the kids rode the bus to New York City—I "flew," high as a kite in March. A decade-long love affair with pot began, ironically, on the steps of the Statue of Liberty.

By my twentieth birthday, I was spending four and five nights a week on a barstool, Southern Comfort in my glass and longing in my eyes. I found companionship in many but comfort in none.

As a radio personality, I traveled from town to town, up and down the dial through my twenties, including a stint at a hard rock station in Detroit, where the shock jock Howard Stern did mornings and I did the afternoon show. As a one-sentence summary of how low my values had plummeted, even Howard once shook his head and said, "Liz, you've got to clean up your act!" It wasn't my on-air act that was in trouble; it was my risky off-air escapades that needed changing.

By the fall of 1981, I found myself in Louisville, Kentucky, playing oldies at an AM station and playing dangerous games with marijuana, speed, cocaine, alcohol, and a promiscuous lifestyle. I'm one of those people who had to fall all the way down to the bottom of the pit before I was forced to look up for help.

Leaning over my pit of despair and extending a hand of friendship was a husband-and-wife team who'd just arrived in town to do the morning show at my radio station. Little did I know that the Lord would use these dear people as my "overnight delivery service."

Although they'd enjoyed much worldly success, what these two talked about most was Jesus Christ. Even more amazing, they seemed to like and accept me, "as is." (Can you imagine what they must have thought when we met? "Now, here's a project!")

But they didn't treat me like a project, a package that needed to be delivered from sin to salvation. They treated me like a friend who needed to know that being delivered was an option. Simply put, they loved me with a love so compelling that I was powerless to resist it.

I remember February 21, 1982, like it was yesterday. It was my seventh Sunday to visit my friends' church, and by then I was singing in the choir. When we closed the service singing "I Have Decided to Follow Jesus," I did just that. Walked right out of the choir loft and down to the baptistry.

The whole alto section gasped. "We thought she was one of us!"

Finally, I was.

God had delivered me from the gates of hell to the gates of heaven—absolutely, positively overnight.

Where would I be without you, Lord?
Thank you for waiting for me to look up.
For wooing me with your irresistible love.
For washing away my sins
and overwhelming me with your mercy and grace.
Help me never forget the price you paid for my delivery.

Approach the Throne

He who is the blessed and only Potentate,
the King of kings and Lord of lords,
who alone has immortality,
dwelling in unapproachable light,
whom no man has seen or can see,
to whom be honor and everlasting power. Amen.

—1 Timothy 6:15–16

Take a second and read those two verses out loud.

Wow. Pretty obvious who's in charge, eh?

Of all the coffee mugs I've ever received, my favorite is a mug my husband gave me that features artwork by Mary Engelbreit and the words *The Queen of Everything*.

Is there some hidden message in this? I may be the Queen of Laughing Heart Farm, but 2.67 acres does not a kingdom make. (Or is that queendom?) In any case, I'm not in charge, and I know it.

The One who's King of everything is Jesus. He is the utmost authority in all the universe. No one is higher, period. No one. He is so powerful that he dwells in "unapproachable light"—light that would not only blind but also destroy mere mortals.

This is not Jesus the meek and mild, the gentle carpenter bent over his woodworking bench. This is the King of kings, seated on the throne of Heaven, "and He has on His robe and on His thigh a name written: KING OF KINGS AND LORD OF LORDS."[2]

You can go no higher than Jesus, the King of kings. He is Supreme. All the earth must obey his commands. He existed before creation, before the beginning of time, and he was in charge then, too.

In the business world, goal-minded sales professionals calling on a corporation are told to ask for the CEO. "Don't quit until you get to the top person," goes the standard advice.

When you call Jesus, not only have you reached the very top, he also answers his own phone! He will not put you on hold or transfer you into a voice-mail system. No one else's call matters more than yours. Though he is King, he is a loving sovereign, not a cruel tyrant. He always has time for you, his loyal subject.

Although you cannot see him with your eyes, you can see him with your heart. And although he has all the powers any despot could hope for, he reaches down to you as friend, brother, husband, savior, the lover of your soul.

So I'll drink from my Queen of Everything coffee mug this morning and laugh. Jesus is King, in charge of it all, and I know it very well.

Lord, forgive me when I think for one minute that
I'm in control of anything. I'm not even in control of me.
Thank goodness you reign from the throne of my heart.
Have thine own way, Lord. Have thine own way.

Joy at Hand

In Your presence is fullness of joy;
At Your right hand are pleasures forevermore.

—Psalm 16·11

My wonderful Bill, first and only husband, is as sweet as honey and genuinely funny, as in ha-ha funny. Those who only see his quiet side never believe me, but it's true: Bill is much funnier than I am. His one-liners are a work of art; his spin on life is clever beyond measure. Blessed woman that I am, I get to bask in his good-natured humor every day of my life.

Considering how long I looked for my life partner, it's only fair that I found a true Prince Charming after such a l-o-n-g line of toads. (If you meet a toad sitting on a barstool, would that make it a *toadstool?!*)

When you and I were seventeen years young, men and marriage were a thrilling, frightening prospect in the distant future. We planned, we prepared, we made lists of all the qualities our mate-for-life was required to have before we'd even give him a second glance. At seventeen, the list was very long indeed. It filled a legal pad, which we happily covered with ink during study hall.

Everything mattered at seventeen.

When I reached twenty-one, still single, I crossed a few things off my list. My dream man no longer needed long, curly eyelashes. I could skip that. He didn't have to drive a Camaro, either. A Nova would do. A Pinto, even.

At twenty-five, I went back to my list and ripped off the bottom half. Stick with the core stuff, I told myself.

By thirty I was working with a Post-it note.

By thirty-two I had one word left—*breathing*.

Bill breathes well. He also has everything I had on my list, except hair. Who cares about such trivialities? I love his slippery scalp and the humorous outlook on life that lives under it.

We've realized that one of the secrets to a happy marriage is remembering the source of our joy, which is not one another. The source of our joy is the Lord. Yes, we share tons of joyous moments, but we don't expect, let alone demand, endless joy-filled moments from each other. Lots of pressure there.

Instead, we turn, hand in hand, toward the same heavenly source, knowing that in the presence of our Savior there's enough joy and pleasure to last a lifetime.

Father, if I made a list
of all the qualities I long to find in a partner
for this life and the next,
you would surpass my every want,
my every need, my every desire.
Bless you for providing my Bill, Father God.
But most of all,
bless you for providing your Son.

LOVABLE YOU

As the Father loved Me,
I also have loved you;
abide in My love.

—JOHN 15:9

Sometimes when we're grumpy and utterly unlovable, it's because we desperately need to *know* we're loved and are unconsciously hoping someone will notice and fix things. Quick.

On a family vacation to New England one summer, Bill found a remarkable way to keep me in good spirits. When I got the least bit cranky or tired, he purred, "Have I told you I love you today?" Ninety-nine percent of the time I would sigh, smile, and say, "Thanks, I needed that." The other one percent, I'd stick out my tongue and say, "Yes, you've told me five times!"

It got so laughable that by the end of the week, if I even felt like getting out of sorts, I'd say, "I know, I know, you love me, you love me!"

When we boarded the plane for our trip home, Bill finally confessed his strategy to me. With some trepidation I asked, "So, how many times did you—"

"At last count, 135."

"Oh." Some of us just can't hear "I love you" enough.

In the same way, God reveals his love for us when we are feeling the least lovable. In my single years, I would sometimes ache with loneliness—genuine, physical pain—and cry out to the walls of my empty little house, "Nobody loves me, Lord; nobody loves me!"

He always responded immediately, not in words for my ears, but in words my heart heard very clearly: *I love you, Liz. I love you.*

Maybe the human love you've received from parents, partners, and/or children has never been enough, never filled you up inside, never seemed to satisfy completely. And no wonder. It's flawed, it's fickle, it's fleeting. Yes, it's also fine—but it's not forever.

God's love is forever love. It's the kind you can abide in and not wonder if it will still be there when you wake up tomorrow. God's love is as solid as the wooden cross that was set into the ground of Golgotha, as solid as the nails that were driven into the flesh of his hands, as solid as the rock that was rolled away from his tomb.

You are loved. Stick that in your heart and abide in it.

Lord, to know that you love me,
even on those days when I am unable to love myself,
is comforting beyond description.
As you have loved me,
help me love others.
Oh, and, Lord?
Have I told you I love you today?

Palm Pilot

Yet I will not forget you.
See, I have inscribed you on the palms of My hands.

—Isaiah 49:15b–16a

One evening a woman came up to me after a presentation and cordially extended her hand. As I greeted her, I couldn't help noticing that clearly written on the palm of her hand were the letters T-A-P-E.

What in the world was that all about? Maybe she was a warden, and it was a reminder to "treat all prisoners equally." Maybe she was taking flying lessons and needed to remember to check "time, altitude, pressure, energy." Wait!! She was a waitress, and that day's special desserts were "tapioca, apple pie, peach cobbler, and éclairs . . ."

My curious mind was on tilt as I debated. *Should I say something or not?* Finally, I couldn't stand it. "What do you mean by 'TAPE'?" I asked.

She looked at her hand, slapped her palm on her forehead, and moaned. "Before I left the house, I was supposed to start the VCR to tape a program for my kids!"

I never would have thought of that, and apparently, she didn't either. Our memories are not always what we want them to be, even when we write things down in the handiest places we can think of. The good news is, God remembers to read his holy hands, and that's precisely where he has written your name.

It isn't cheating for him to write it there, as it was when I scribbled $X+Y=Z$ on my palm before a high school algebra test. The Lord writes your name there for *your* sake, not for his, so he can show you absolute proof: "See, I didn't forget you. Your name is right here on the palms of my hands." So personal, so visual, such an unforgettable image.

Those same palms were pierced with nails on Calvary, leaving scars to prove once again that he has not forgotten you. He said to the doubting apostle Thomas, "Reach your finger here, and look at My hands. . . . Do not be unbelieving, but believing."[3]

Believe, beloved.

Read it in his hands. Read it in his Word.

He will never forget you, always forgive you, never forsake you.

Lord, that you would be willing to write my name, not only
in the Book of Life but also on your own nail-
scarred hands . . . such knowledge is too much for me!

Running . . . and
Running . . . and
Running . . .

Do you not know that those who run in a race all run,
but one receives the prize?
Run in such a way that you may obtain it.

—*1 Corinthians 9:24*

At a weekend conference, a Houston woman tucked a colorful child's block in my hand. "I know it must be hard to find time to exercise on the road. Maybe this will help."

I glanced down at the note attached to the little toy:

1. *Place block on floor.*

2. *Run around it two times.*

3. *Sit down and relax. After all, you just ran*
   around the block twice!

Tee-hee. My kind of exercise, to be sure.

Some women really get into working out, like my friend Audrey from New York, a fifty-plus *fox*. For years I suspected healthy eating and good genes, until she admitted to me, "I have a personal trainer over twice weekly. He's thirty-seven and *fine*." (Hey, why not have a workout room with a view?)

For the rest of us, though, we'd really like to find a trainer who would run around the block *for* us. Sign *him* up for all those aerobics classes. Make *her* sweat to the oldies. Oh, our spirits are willing, even eager, but our bodies are merely amused.

Lately I've noticed that mornings aren't so much "rise and shine" as they are "cries and whine." Dale admits, "I used to leap out of bed. Now I roll to the edge and push myself up to a sitting position. The next big challenge is to stand up and walk to the bathroom without all my bones creaking and snapping so loud that I wake up my husband!"

I do wish I'd started some kind of regular fitness routine sooner. I keep telling my children, "Start walking now! Make exercise a habit!"

"But, Mom!" they whine in unison. "Exercise isn't a habit for *you*!"

Guilty as charged.

I really am trying. Every single day, I tell myself, "Go for a walk! Go for a walk! Take a break for twenty minutes and do it!" Then when I do, I'm so worn out, I can't walk back. I start looking for neighbors to flag down and drive me home. Pitiful.

I'm grateful to be married to a man who understands. Bill strapped on his old running shoes one evening, reminding me, "Before we married, I used to jog five miles every night." (I fought the urge to remind him that was also the *last* time he'd gone jogging.) Mere minutes later Bill came panting back through the doorway, bug-eyed and bleeding.

His story, told between deep gulps of air, was much more dramatic than the novel I was reading. He'd made it two blocks, tripped over a tree root sticking out of the sidewalk, flown through the air in middle-aged disgrace, and landed on his bum knee (all men have a bum knee, even if they never played contact sports). Dogs nearby started barking, porch lights were flicked on, and Bill hobbled home a bloody mess.

Bless him, the man really was in pain. I squirted some Bactine on his knee and sent him off to bed grumbling about cracks in the sidewalk and dim street lighting.

We're both grateful that when the Lord asked us to run toward the prize, it wasn't a blue ribbon or a gold medal he had in mind. Rather it was "an imperishable crown,"[4] the ultimate prize of eternal life.

Lord Jesus, you know I'm a poor excuse for an athlete.
Yet I promise to run with all my heart toward you.
When I stumble, help me rise to run again.
When I skin my knees, clean me up and put me back on track.
Thank you for standing at the finish line, cheering me on.

Thanks Giving

Therefore by Him let us continually offer the sacrifice of praise to God,
that is, the fruit of our lips, giving thanks to His name.

—Hebrews 13:15

Whatever season waits outside your window—a white and wintry morning, a bright spring day, a sultry summer afternoon, or a crisp autumn evening—imagine for a moment that every day is Thanksgiving. Because, for those of us who love God, it is. Especially when he gives us a gift as precious as a child.

I was a newlywed of eight months, wrestling with a big, fat turkey, when impending motherhood knocked on my door. I was too preoccupied with getting my first Thanksgiving dinner on the table to even notice all the telltale symptoms.

It was almost 2:00—Zero Hour—when Bill's mom, dad, and grandmother were scheduled to arrive. "Bill!" I called out, dashing toward the living room. "Please tell me you vacuumed when I wasn't paying attention!"

"Wh-what? Huh?" Bill struggled to sit up from his prone position on the couch, while I slammed the vacuum on and shoved it dangerously close to his bare feet. "Honey, I'm sorry," he said, rubbing the sleep out of his eyes.

"Too late now, buster!" I hollered over the roar of the vacuum. "Celebrating Thanksgiving at our house was your idea, remember? Your idea, your family, and you didn't even help. This is the last time I try to impress those three, believe me!"

I yanked the plug out of the wall to move to the next room, still breathing threats, when suddenly I froze. Someone was gently knocking on the glass of our front door, mere feet away.

Realization and dread poured over me like gravy on mashed potatoes. Handing Bill the vacuum, I opened the front door with a sickly grin and faced the inevitable. "Hi, folks." I swallowed a hard lump of regret. "Happy Thanksgiving."

"Really?" My mother-in-law raised an eyebrow as she walked past me, casserole in hand.

"Sorry you caught me having a hissy fit," I continued, with a weary sigh. "It's been a . . . challenging day." Why was I so cranky?

We had plenty of time to smooth things over, since the turkey didn't come out of the oven until nearly six o'clock. I, however, couldn't eat a bite. Couldn't even bear the smell of it. For a woman who loves to eat as much as I do, this was a rare moment indeed. "Not even a slice of my delicious chocolate pie?" Nanny asked, and I felt my stomach flip over.

"No thanks," I said weakly and rose to clear the table. Just what I needed—some intestinal flu thing for the long holiday weekend ahead. Exhausted, I excused myself to stretch out on the couch while dear Bill handled kitchen duty. When his family murmured their good-byes, I offered a wimpy wave from my prone position in the living room, afraid to risk standing.

"Honey, are you okay?" Bill knelt beside the sofa and looked intently at my chalk-white face.

"I'll be all right," I mumbled, but even I was not convinced.

By Saturday morning, the queasiness had settled in to stay, even after plenty of sleep, no cooking, a quiet house, and a day off work.

There *was* one possible explanation, outrageous as it seemed. After a quick trip to the drugstore that morning, I spent a little extra time in the rest room with a home pregnancy test, feeling like a chemist and shaking like a leaf.

Minutes later, Bill and I sat at the kitchen table and watched with fear and trembling as the little vial changed color, and the truth changed our lives forever.

It was neither romantic nor touching, but it *is* what I said: "It's a go, Higgs!"

We were indeed with child.

Two old people, latecomers to marriage, wed to our careers, strangers to parenting, thrilled to the tips of our toes, giving thanks all over the place.

What is the greatest earthly blessing the Lord has given you, in any season of your life? Let this day be one of thanks giving, sis. No turkeys necessary, just a heart full of gratitude.

Oh, Lord, how well I remember that sacred day!
This morning, and every morning, let me thank you anew
for all the blessings you shower on an undeserving
(and sometimes ungrateful) child like me.
Most of all, we give thanks for Jesus.

Got Grandkids?

Children's children are a crown to the aged . . .

—*Proverbs 17:6a NIV*

If you're a young woman, grandchildren may be the last thing on your mind. But for those of us whose children are moving through the teen years and beyond, the hope of holding a baby again some-day is a sweet promise indeed. Barb from Ohio thinks the best part of grandparenting is being able to truly enjoy the grandkids "and be amused by what they say and do, instead of being embarrassed!"

Case in point: Bill and I went on a dream tenth-anniversary trip to Scotland, leaving our two children, then seven and eight, in the very able hands of a dear friend. A visit to their paternal grandpar-ents was scheduled for the middle of our bonnie holiday abroad. Around lunchtime in Dumfries, Scotland (five hours earlier back home), we found a bright red phone box and started shoving pounds (the coin kind) into the telephone, trying to make a long-distance connection to Kentucky.

No sooner did Bill's parents answer the phone, than the timer ran out and a beeper sounded, indicating it was time to feed the phone again. (Picture a woman my size leaning out of a phone booth shouting, "More pounds! More pounds!")

Our conversation was disjointed at best, but it soon became clear there'd been an "incident" concerning our daughter, Lillian. "Lillian did not have a good day at school" was the first clue. A garbled phrase followed, then the operator jumped on the line and more pounds got jammed into the coin slot, just in time to hear my mother-in-law say, ". . . picked her up at the principal's office after she . . .," and the line went dead again.

Several British pounds (and poundings) later, the phone cooperated long enough for us to grasp the whole sordid story.

Maybe it was May, spring fever, end of the year, we don't know what all, but our daughter had the urge to try something that would *really* get someone's attention, so . . . she . . . uh, pointed at another child with a finger not generally considered polite to use for pointing.

Oh my.

Please understand, the child had *no earthly idea* what such a gesture meant, but she quickly discovered that pointing like that made the adults at her nice Christian school practically swoon. By the time our in-laws had picked her up in the carpool line, four or five notes were sticking out of her book bag, and Lillian herself was proudly proclaiming, "Guess what I did at school today?"

The silence across the ocean was deafening. "Mom," I said wearily, "I hope you know she didn't learn such a vulgar gesture from *us.*"

Long pause. Too long. "Well, we didn't think so. Kids just pick up these things." My mother-in-law, a veteran of public school teaching, has been around the block a few times. "In fact, Lillian was so proud of herself, she couldn't wait to tell the couple next door all about it. Complete with a demonstration."

Gulp. "You mean those nice people who used to own the Christian bookstore?"

"The very ones. Actually, they thought it was hysterical."

Great. My daughter has torn our parental reputation to shreds and had the neighbors rolling in the aisles, all in one day.

No doubt about it, children keep their parents humble . . . and their grandparents amused.

Father God, does my foolish behavior amuse you, too?
I pray so, Lord, because sometimes I do the wrong thing
without meaning to.
Forgive me when I fail as a parent,
or falter as your child.
If I have the blessing of being a grandmother someday,
remind me of the grace that was extended to me
as both parent and child,
over and over and over.

Sound Investment

Houses and riches are an inheritance from fathers,
But a prudent wife is from the LORD.

—PROVERBS 19:14

Balancing your checkbook today, dearie? Checking your investments online, perhaps?

Unfortunately, I'm great at earning and spending but not so good at saving.

I actually thought a "portfolio" was a leather pouch that held sketches and paintings. So, when my banker inquired the status of my investment portfolio, I said, "Are you kidding? It's empty, baby. My artistic abilities are zilch."

He quietly closed his file folder and thanked me for stopping by.

My insurance agent, on the other hand, took a deep breath and tried to explain it all to me. After an hour of dizzying statistics and fine print legalese, I sighed, "So basically, we give you all the money we have left at the end of each year, and you try not to spend it all before we hit retirement, is that it?"

She smiled and took my check. We now had a portfolio. Imagine that! A couple who thought "no-load" meant a washer that emptied the wet clothes into the dryer by itself ended up playing the stock market like a violin.

When the quarterly statement arrives, we go straight to the bottom line: "Oh good, it went up!" or "Oh no, it went down!" Then we throw it away.

I'm amused by the ads that tout, "Make your money work for you." I think our money just got downsized out of a job. Sometimes the only activity on the statement is the thirty dollar service fee.

You could probably earn the same yield by stuffing your money in your couch. Unless your kids are still jumping on it, in which case a coffee can works fine, too. Beware the gold-embossed investment folios with this little verse discreetly printed in the corner: "Cast but a glance at riches, and they are gone."[5] Trust me, this is a portent of things to come.

I'm just grateful that Bill and I could even come to a point of agreement about how to invest our limited resources. To say that the two of us have similar philosophies about money would be like suggesting that Dolly and Twiggy have almost the same measurements.

Bill is tight and I'm . . . not. He likes to count money; I like to give it away. He likes to save money; I like to spend it, though I'm on catalog probation until further notice.

Maybe you, like me, relate to the woman whose mother kept a red ink pen in the glove compartment. When her mom returned home from a shopping spree and was safely parked in the driveway, she'd pull out all the tags and mark them down herself.

Love it.

For those of us who always thought our spiritual gift was shopping, there *is* hope, sis: marry a frugal man or a very savvy stockbroker. And pray.

> *Oh, Lord, your Word says a great deal about money*
> *and stewardship and wise, prudent investments.*
> *Give me the strength this day*
> *to throw away the catalogs and department store fliers,*
> *and invest in your kingdom.*
> *My heart is there, Lord.*
> *Let my treasure be also.*

Age Anxiety

Those who are planted in the house of the LORD
Shall flourish in the courts of our God.
They shall still bear fruit in old age;
They shall be fresh and flourishing.

—*Psalm 92:13–14*

Feel like confessing your age today, eh? I'll go first.

The day I turned forty dawned like any other summer Sunday morning: It was hot and I was bothered. I slapped off the alarm clock, whining to no one in particular, "Help! I'm forty and I can't get up."

My children offered zero comfort. Ages five and seven at the time, they were too young to buy me presents and too old not to notice my advancing age (prompted by their father, of course). "Happy Birthday, Mom!" they sang out as I trudged down the steps. "Golly, you *do* look older!"

The morning went downhill from there. At church, it was lots of good-natured ribbing in the vestibule after the service. Oh sure, ha-ha-ha, over the hill, thank you very much. By two o'clock it was Depression City, thanks to a silent phone, an empty mailbox (even if it *was* Sunday), and the absence of gifts from my husband ("Honey, you said you didn't need anything!").

The only party at my house was a pity party. The only card I got said, "Once you hit forty, you gotta be careful . . . At your age, it's hard to get new parts."

Harrumph. I crawled off to bed for a midafternoon nap, hoping I'd wake up a happier woman—or thirty again.

When I opened my eyes an hour later, I was still a decade older but well rested enough to face the truth: The Big 4-0 had arrived, and there was nothing I could do but accept it. Yes, even celebrate it.

I took a deep breath, leaped out of bed, and headed for the family room. "I'm up!" I called out. And finally, I was.

Maybe you're facing twenty and suddenly realizing, as the song says, "You're not a kid anymore."

Maybe you're staring thirty in the face and don't like what you see.

Maybe it's the Big 5-0 that you're approaching with fear and trepidation. Or perhaps sixty is resting heavily on your shoulders. Or seventy. Or eighty.

These are milestones, not millstones, beloved. Celebrate them with joy and abandon. In the poem below, substitute the age that fits you right now, and see if this little rhyme of mine won't lift your spirits as you prepare for new vistas.

So it's <u>forty</u> you've been dreading?
O'er the hill you'll soon be heading?
Take a tip from those of us who've seen the view:
It's a joyful celebration
Of the sudden realization
That you finally have permission to be *you!*

Atta, girl. Feeling better?

I'm so grateful, Father, to simply be alive.
Help me celebrate every day and every age,
knowing that as each year passes
I am one step closer
to standing in your holy presence.

In the Long Run

Surely every man walks about like a shadow;
Surely they busy themselves in vain.

—Psalm 39:6

Busy, are you? Me, too. Too too.

Whenever I take on a new challenge, my husband Bill says, "That's fine, but what activity are you going to drop in order to make this one happen?"

"Drop?" I ask, with that hand-in-the-cookie-jar look on my face. "Gosh, I wasn't going to drop anything. I figured I'd just squeeze it in during the commercials."

The time management books I've seen (and believe me, this isn't one of them!) encourage us to maximize every single waking moment. They give us exercises to do at our desk, Scripture verses to memorize at red lights, language tapes to listen to while we jog, thank-you postcards to carry in our purse for a spare second while standing in line at the bank. Sure, we can accomplish more, but the real question is, "Why?" Is all the energy output worth the emotional input?

The one thing women want *more* of is the one variable we can't change: *time.* Yet, whether we look back to biblical times or to the turn of any century, we've always had the same number of seconds in a minute, minutes in an hour, and hours in a day—even if we called them something else.

Psychologist Dr. Kevin Leman insists, "Getting your priorities straight and sticking to them is one of the most difficult tasks in life."[6] What makes it easier for me is consciously listening to God's voice, my husband's voice, and my own voice, seeking to create harmony rather than a dissonant chord. This requires ignoring the voices of media and peer pressure and filtering out the "you shoulds" from well-meaning but ill-informed sources.

Some questions worth asking ourselves might be:

- Will this activity matter one week from today? One month? One year?
- Is there someone who does it better than I do, to whom I might delegate this activity?
- Does it satisfy a heartfelt need for me or someone I love very much?
- What are the ramifications if I *don't* do it?
- What are the outcomes if I *do* do it?

This exercise might be a little much for considering whether you should take out the trash. The answer there is yes! But for any activity that will require even a modest drain on your time/money/energy/emotional resources, answering these simple questions could provide the pause you need to reconsider and say, "I'll pass."

I know it's foolish to pray for more time, Lord.
You've given me more than enough to work with.
Instead, I would ask for the wisdom
to spend my time more productively,
and the discernment to know
the value of no
and the price of yes.

WEIGHING IN

Let me be weighed on honest scales,
That God may know my integrity.

—JOB 31:6

So, beloved, did you weigh yourself this morning? Was it ugly? Are you hurting?

More tears have been shed over expanding waistlines than all of life's other challenges combined, including departing sweethearts and declining bank accounts.

Each day brings a new diet book, and magazine racks shout monthly, "Lose Twenty Pounds in Twenty Days!" We buy it, we try it, we cry when it doesn't work. Everyone is dieting, but the only thing we're losing is our self-esteem.

My first diet was at age ten, followed by dozens more in later years. I was the classic yo-yo dieter: up and down, up and down. I had to try everything, had to hit rock bottom emotionally before I woke up.

That "wake-up call" came soon after my thirtieth birthday. Weary of looking for love in all the wrong places and trying to diet my way into some man's arms, I threw out every scale in the house (both the big kind you stand on and the little ones that weigh food) and announced to the world, "This is the Liz-that-is!"

Know what? The mountains didn't crumble and the earth didn't stop spinning. What *did* happen was that I finally rested in God's complete and loving acceptance of me, big hips and all. That's what helped me accept myself. That's what made the difference.

This very morning, thousands of women across America are still trying to diet their way to happiness. Not only big women, mind you, but medium-size and thin women. We tell ourselves that if we "just lose ten pounds" (or twenty, forty, sixty pounds), we will look better, feel better, even be better people.

So much for complete and loving acceptance.

Too often we postpone joy until we are, say, a size 10. I've *been* a size 10 and was not more joyful at that size than I am now. "Thin" does not guarantee health, happiness, or a husband. Today, and every day, you need to be assured that you are a woman of immeasurable worth and great beauty, "as is," not "when."

This does not mean giving up, nor does it mean living in denial. It's simply an acknowledgment of our physiological differences and an acceptance of the bodies we've been given. More than acceptance, it's a celebration!

Lord Jesus, weigh my heart.
Is it full of love for you
and overflowing with compassion for others?
Let me rejoice, then, in having an XXXL heart.
And let me come to a place of peace
about my body, at any size.

All (Green) Thumbs

Is gardening on your to-do list today, sis?

I kill plants on contact, but my precious mother was quite the gardener.

A bit of history: I was born in my mother's forty-third year. I was a surprise. A shock. A disaster, even. She'd already mothered five children, one right after another. Then, after enjoying nine long years of peace from pregnancy, it was back to maternity clothes for Mom. She was mortified. None of her Garden Club friends were having babies in their forties, for heaven's sake.

After I arrived on the scene, Mom had to fit in her gardening whenever she could, often at odd hours. One starlit summer night I called out the back door looking for her. "Mom! M-o-m-m-m!" No sound, no movement. Had she stumbled in the asparagus patch? Was she lost among the sunflowers?

I found a flashlight and bravely ventured out into the spooky garden filled with shadows that didn't resemble my mother at all. After several frantic minutes of searching, I discovered her on the far edge of our property, precariously balanced on a steep embankment, planting marigolds by the light of the moon.

At least I always knew where to find her. Arriving home from school each day, I'd find her bent over her poppies or plucking petunias. That round, blue-jeaned bottom pointing skyward was a very comforting sight. Years later, when I passed a garden center displaying a decorative plywood figure of a bent-over woman in polka-dot pantaloons, I cried out in astonishment, "That's my mother!"

Even at that young age, I suspected it was my mother's overriding need to *escape* that drove her off to her garden with increasing frequency. Escape what, I did not know. Rather than ask, I simply sat in the house and missed her company.

Of course, I was very proud of my mother's gifts and talents. She could take three flowers, or five or seven (the pros always use an odd number of stems), and create a floral design that captured blue ribbons and filled our house with beauty. Gardening gurus from far and wide came to our Front Street house to gawk at my mother's handiwork, which swelled my young heart with pride.

But even so, I missed her when she was lost in her garden books or hiding in her flower beds. What child doesn't long for undivided attention from her parents?

It's taken me a lifetime to comprehend the truth: Our parents can never shower us with love as God can. No matter how great their affection or how focused their attention, only the love of our heavenly Father satisfies our hungry hearts.

How easy it is to blame an adult child's misery on less-than-ideal parenting. And how unproductive that can be. Because we cannot change our past or how our parents treated us.

What we *can* do is turn to our heavenly Father for complete and unconditional love. Now. And pour his love into our children, knowing they will never be lonely if they know their true Father.

> *Lord Jesus, sometimes it hurts to remember*
> *an empty house and hours alone*
> *What comfort to know that you were there*
> *every minute,*
> *watering me with your love*
> *even as my dear mother watered her garden.*
> *We both grew, the garden and me.*
> *And with that growth came understanding*
> *and a blossoming sense of peace.*

No Sweat

For physical training is of some value, but godliness has value for all things, holding promise for both the present life and the life to come.

—1 Timothy 4:8 niv

When it comes to exercise, I may hate squat thrusts . . . but I love to dance.

From my toddler days when my older sisters taught me how to do the twist at their slumber parties, I delighted in the way my body felt when it moved across a polished wooden floor, music pounding in the background.

In my midtwenties, I showed up for my first jazz dance class wearing the standard black leotard and tights (workout gear was not as slinky and colorful in those days) and the soft, black ballet slippers. Plunking down my money, I signed my name to the day's roster and stepped into the dance studio.

Sunlight poured through the windows, and the wood beneath my feet felt warm. The music began. Rhythmic, energetic, magnetic. My body responded instinctively. Swaying, stretching, bending. It felt wonderful to move to music again.

I hung in the back row with the other beginners, carefully watching the women in front, mimicking their every move. One, two, step, step, lunge, back, slide, slide. I'm a fairly quick study and soon could feel my pulse pick up at the excitement of doing something so right, so good for my body.

Then it happened. My eyes caught the instructor following my every move. She was smirking. No, make that *laughing*.

I glanced around the room. Had I missed something amusing? I turned back to her with a quizzical look on my face, and she put words to my fears: "You look so funny when you move." The rest of the class giggled and kept dancing.

My heart was broken. I finished the class that day, but I never went back.

What a shame that I allowed one insensitive instructor's pronouncement to rob my joy! Today the older-but-wiser Liz knows better. Movement is all about having fun and doing good things for your body, not about looking good while doing it. Though my too-small black leotard is history, my new walking shoes are a perfect fit.

Walking is my favorite exercise because . . .

1. I don't need any special equipment, just my feet (which, to be sure, are very special size-10 equipment!).

2. I can walk anywhere, anytime, without planning ahead, joining a club, or driving somewhere first.

3. It's free.

4. It requires absolutely no squat thrusts.

I'm going for a walk today. How 'bout you?

As my feet move forward, Lord, let my thoughts move heavenward.
Fill me with enough energy to both walk and pray,
to take in the bounty of your creation
and the beauty of you.
Please whisper a word of encouragement when I grow weary,
and a "Well done, daughter," when I finish.
Thanks for always walking with me, Jesus.

FLIGHT OF FANCY

But God has chosen the foolish things of the world
to put to shame the wise,
and God has chosen the weak things of the world
to put to shame the things which are mighty.

—1 CORINTHIANS 1:27

If I ever doubt my foolishness or my weakness, the memory of one unusual air travel experience comes to mind and keeps me humble.

I'd just walked into the passenger terminal at the Indianapolis airport and was looking for somewhere to land until they called my flight. Almost every seat in the waiting area was filled, but at the end of one of the rows were two seats joined together on a T-shaped base. On one of those seats sat a very thin young lady who barely took up half her side.

Perfect! I'd have room for both my hips. I sat down and greeted her warmly. "Lovely day, isn't it?"

Then it happened: When I leaned over to reach my luggage, she suddenly stood up.

Did you ever ride a seesaw as a child? Then you know what happens if the other kid gets off too fast . . .

Seconds later, I was shouting out something like "G-r-r-a-a-a-k-k!"

I turned the entire double seat completely over sideways and went tumbling, tails over teacups.

This attracted the attention of the men behind the ticket counter, who rushed over to try and help me get up. They could not. Not because of my size (there *were* three of them) and not because I was pinned under the chair, but because I was laughing so hard.

Have you ever laughed on the floor . . . on your face? It makes a humping, wheezing sound. "Wheeesh!" Which really concerned them. "Ma'am, shall we call a doctor?" That just made it worse. "Wheee-heeesh!"

Finally they got the chair up. They got me up. I carefully sat back down on the T-shaped seat—in the middle. That was when I realized the waiting area was stone silent. More than one hundred people were obviously thinking, *That is the funniest thing I have ever seen!* But they dared not laugh out loud. Instead they hid behind newspapers or looked around the room—anywhere but at me.

Meanwhile, I could not stop laughing. Not with a scene like that dancing around in my head. A big woman in a black coat, flying without a broom? *Wheeesh!*

Finally, I got out my compact to see if my lipstick had survived my unscheduled flight. Looking in the mirror I caught a glimpse of another larger woman behind me. Her lips were so tightly pinched together to keep from laughing, she looked like she'd swallowed a cat.

I sized her up as a sister immediately, leaned toward her, and whispered, "I'm just thankful I didn't flip that little woman up in the air."

That was all it took. "Wheesh!" In stereo. People would not even look in our direction. I may never see her again, but that woman and I are now joined at the funny bone for life.

If you're planning any unexpected trips today, remember the wise words of Ethel Barrymore: "You grow up the day you have your first real laugh . . . at yourself."

Sometimes, Lord, I do the silliest things.
Help me laugh instead of cry, or blush, or hide.
Give me the grace to stand to my feet with a smile on my face . . .
humbled but happy, foolish yet wise enough to know
the power of laughing at myself.

GUIDANCE COUNSELOR

Nevertheless I am continually with You;
You hold me by my right hand.
You will guide me with Your counsel . . .

—PSALM 73:23–24A

I was waiting nervously on a hospital gurney, about to be wheeled into surgery for an emergency appendectomy, when a nurse approached me with a three-foot needle. (Okay, it was more like five inches, but it *looked* like three feet.)

"I'll need to insert this IV into your wrist," she said matter-of-factly and began stabbing at the veins in my wrist. The pain of this exercise was excruciating for my wimpy self, a woman with a minus-ten threshold of pain.

"Oops!" the nurse said with a slight laugh. "Let's try again." Ouch! More very pointed pain.

"Third time's a charm," she promised, as I looked the other way and began praying earnestly. *Make the pain go away, Lord. Now, Lord. No, yesterday, Lord!*

He was listening, and his response was immediate. *I am with you in the pain, Liz. I've been there, and I am here.* He didn't take the pain itself away, yet he made my endurance of it possible because

I knew I was not alone. How like a Counselor, to be with us in our pain and offer encouragement through the process.

Earthly counselors can be heaven-sent too. I spent a long, painful yet productive year in a therapist's office and learned that the greatest gift a counselor gives you is the gift of listening without judging. A good Christian counselor offers guidance, support, a steady hand, a safe harbor. Then, there's *the* Counselor, the Lord himself, who is by nature superior in every way to his earthly counterparts. He not only listens but can also extend forgiveness. He not only guides; he also leads by perfect example. Not to mention that his office hours are eternal, you never need an appointment, and his invoices are always marked, "Paid in Full." A mighty Counselor is he!

> Lord, remind me to call you first when I need counseling,
> knowing that my hope for recovery lies in you.
> Help me also not to be afraid to reach out
> to your earthly servants,
> knowing that together
> we can lean on you for heavenly guidance.

POLISHED GEMS

The silver-haired head is a crown of glory,
If it is found in the way of righteousness.

—*Proverbs 16:31*

Have you found your first gray hair yet, sis?

Or your tenth? Or—be honest—does the gray outnumber the rest?

Gray hairs may be "the splendor of the old,"[7] but Dale from Illinois doesn't think they're so splendid: "I have spent many moments plucking the gray hairs around my hairline, but who knows what I'm missing in the back! Then I noticed a gray hair in my eyebrows—do I pluck or use more eyebrow pencil?"

Give up a perfectly healthy eyebrow hair? Revlon to the rescue! I just wish they made eyebrow pencils to match your hair coloring lotion. Wouldn't it be grand if hair coloring kits came with coordinating eyebrow pencils taped to the lid, "Free with Purchase"?

I like to ask women in my audience, "How many of you have no idea what your natural hair color is?" Honest hands pop up all over the room, followed by gasps from their friends who never knew the truth. These are women who, like me, started out using "Sun-In" at the pool during the sixties, then graduated to Lady Clairol 121, and finally switched to L'Oreal because we're worth it.

I sported blond locks for the first forty years of my life but found that the blond and the gray were starting to fight for attention up there. Then, along with thousands of other American women, I opted for red hair for a season and was delighted with the results. Why be salt-and-pepper when you can be paprika? Now I'm back to blond until I have enough confidence (and naturally graying hair) to go gray all the way.

Maybe it's that word *gray* that's the problem. Effective immediately, let's start calling them *silver* hairs. Gray conjures up images of dark, gloomy days and boring business suits. Silver sounds much more eye-catching: silver dollars, silver certificates, sterling silver, silver jewelry. Instead of coloring our hair, let's just polish it!

Lord Jesus, let me not be dismayed by gray hairs;
let me be encouraged that I've lived long enough to see them.
Your Word celebrates the silver-headed among us.
When it's my time to shine, Jesus,
let me shine for you,
starting with the very hairs of my head.

A Heap o' Trouble

Two are better than one,
because they have a good return for their work:
If one falls down,
his friend can help him up.
But pity the man who falls
and has no one to help him up!

—*Ecclesiastes 4:9–10 NIV*

Author Luci Swindoll admits that laughter was such a part of her childhood. "It wasn't a good day unless you fell over in a heap."

I don't think my experience was exactly what Luci had in mind.

One summer night, thanks to new blacktop on our rural driveway, I had to park several blocks away and walk home. In the dark. Through a cornfield.

Finally, only a hundred yards or so stretched between me and our dear, dilapidated barn. One more fence and I was home free. A hasty inspection brought bad news: The fencing was wire and had no gate. Launching my larger-than-average body over sharp metal seemed foolish, even dangerous, but launch it I would.

I found a discarded wooden crate, prayed it would hold me, and climbed on. The absence of splintering sounds buoyed my confidence. Guessing the distance and hoping for a soft landing, I took a deep breath and leaped over the fence, high heels in hand.

Thwommpp!

It was a soft landing, all right. Too soft. Squishy, even. I was soon up to my knees in whatever it was. Not manure, thank goodness, but not dirt, either. Too soft for leaves, too warm for sand. Oh my . . . it couldn't be . . .

I had landed in our neighbor's compost heap! It had to be four feet deep and ten feet wide. Getting out was going to be problematic at best. One wrong move and I could tumble facefirst into the muck. Yuck.

"Help!" I whispered faintly to no one in particular. My arms were the only thing I could move safely, so I flapped them up and down like a big chicken, hoping someone, anyone, might happen by and rescue me. "Help, help," I said again with less enthusiasm. Who was I kidding? Nobody visits their compost heap in the dark. Except . . .

No! I refused to think about the various critters that probably spent many a happy night in that heap. I was in the midst of devising the best route of escape from my compost prison when, out of the corner of my eye, I spied a light bobbing along in my direction. Just a few feet off the ground, seemingly attached to nothing, it slowly grew brighter, weaving along an eerie path of its own making, hovering in the night like a . . .

"Aahhhhh!"

"Liz? Are you okay?"

I almost dropped seatfirst into the compost. My beloved Bill had come to rescue me. "Oh, honey, help me out," I stammered, feeling weepy and lightheaded with relief.

Bill put down his big flashlight, practically lifted me out of the mountain of compost—no easy feat—and brushed the worst of it off my legs.

"How did you hear me way out here?" My voice was shaking like a woman who'd just had a close encounter with an alien.

"I *didn't* hear you, Liz. I saw your car pass by the end of our driveway thirty minutes ago and knew you should've been home by now." Even in the darkness, I could see his grin. "I figured you'd try to find a shortcut."

Hardly noticing the sticks and stones tearing up my panty hose as I tiptoed toward the house, I sent up a silent prayer of thanks for my ever-watchful mate and recalled the verse from Ecclesiastes 4 that has appeared on most of our anniversary cards: *Two are better than one. If one falls down, his friend can help him up.*

Amen to that, girlfriend. Especially when you fall in a heap.

Thanks for being there, Lord.
Guiding me to safety as always,
even when I'm headed for a heap o' trouble.
Your grace alone is my assurance
of soft landings and happy endings.
Eventually.

YES, INDEED

For all the promises of God in Him are Yes,
and in Him Amen, to the glory of God through us.

—2 CORINTHIANS 1:20

Yes, yes, yes, sister! That's God's word for you today.

Picture the scene: I was bent over, digging in a box for additional items for my book table. My least flattering side was on full display when a retreat attendee stopped by my table and made a muffled request. Since my ears were under the table with me, I couldn't quite understand what she was saying, but raised my head and assured her, "Whatever you need, the answer is *yes!*"

She responded immediately, "What a great promise!"

Indeed. But it's not original with me. That's what the Word of God says about Jesus: In him the promises of God are yes. Amen, that's right, so be it, yea, and verily.

Grasp this concept: Whenever you read a promise in Scripture (there are hundreds of them), such as when Jesus said, "Whatever things you ask in prayer, believing, you will receive,"[8] just add yes! Punch your fist in the air, if you like. Clap your hands, slap the table—whatever action feels like yes will do nicely. The key is that because of Jesus and his work on the cross, the promises are not empty; they are fulfilled; they are yes.

Jesus said, "When the Helper comes, whom I shall send to you from the Father, the Spirit of truth who proceeds from the Father, He will testify of Me."[9] And of course, not long after he spoke this, the Holy Spirit did come at Pentecost, which is yet another yes from God, another promise come true, another verification, another reason to trust his Word.

When I am in a moment of deep prayer, feeling close to God and in tune with his Spirit, I find myself nodding a lot. "Yes, Lord, yes!" We know he can be trusted because what he promises becomes reality.

What a different picture this paints from the "thou shalt not" God that many people imagine him to be. To be sure, those "thou shalt nots" are still in Scripture and still his commands. But the emphasis in the New Testament is on the "thou shalls" and on the fulfillment of his many promises to those who love him.

God has said "Yes!" to you.

How will you answer him today?

Lord, help me focus on what you've promised me,
because it makes obedience so much easier.
Obedience flows from love,
from yes,
from agreement that to obey your commands
is not only right but also good.
To you, Lord, I say yes!

MEAN GREEN

Do not weary yourself to gain wealth,
Cease from your consideration of it.
When you set your eyes on it, it is gone.
For wealth certainly makes itself wings,
Like an eagle that flies toward the heavens.

—*PROVERBS 23:4–5 NASB*

When it comes to cash, there never seems to be enough of it. As Richard Armour said, "That money talks, I'll not deny; I heard it once; it said, 'Good-bye!'"

My experience is that when payday comes, the check goes in the bank, the balance looks terrific, I spend twenty minutes writing checks to pay the bills, and the balance is right back where it was when I started. In theory, one would think that if we earned just a little more money, it would solve that problem. My own life tells me that when we make a little more, we spend a little more—sometimes before we even earn it.

When frugal Bill and I married, we set up housekeeping on a property so small that we didn't even need a lawn mower. Cutting the grass meant wielding a Weed Eater for ten minutes and we were done. Money was tight in the early years, and on paper there was no way Bill and I could pull off starting a business *and* starting a family, financially.

But we did it. Sometimes it meant borrowing money from a loved one for a season or paying back our obligations on time but v-e-r-y slowly. Most of the time it meant doing without. Peanut butter was a daily fare (until it got too pricey), and eating out meant we split a Happy Meal at McDonald's, and our baby got the prize!

For fun, we went for long drives up and down the neighboring streets in the evening while Matthew snoozed in his car seat. As the houses got bigger and more expensive, we marveled at their size and guessed at their value. After a few blocks, my eyes started gleaming, green with envy. So, to keep our covetousness in check, we intentionally turned down streets where the houses and yards were smaller and the cars at the curb were older.

Finally, we pulled into our own driveway and said, "Oh, what a mansion! Thank you, God, for our beautiful home!" It was more cottage than castle, but it was ours (and the bank's), and we were most grateful.

Lord, how easy it is to put my trust in riches
and my faith in finances . . . and how foolish.
Help me enjoy your gifts with a spirit of gratitude
and let go of any longing for more wealth,
more security, more stuff.
Your provision for us
is enough, Lord Jesus.

Plant Food

I am the vine, you are the branches.
He who abides in Me, and I in him, bears much fruit;
for without Me you can do nothing.

—JOHN 15:5

About the only things I can grow are geraniums. Big, showy red ones are my favorite. One spring I went all out and bought the biggest geranium plants in captivity. Make a circle with your arms and you get the idea: *big.* Two of them, one for each side of the steps up to the front porch, which I was going to plant in two even bigger clay pots, so huge they looked like they belonged in the land of Lilliput.

I "walked" the empty clay pots into place at the foot of the steps and positioned them just where I wanted them. Then, I gingerly picked up one of the gargantuan geraniums in order to ease it down inside the pot a bit and see how much dirt it was going to take to fill the pot.

That was my first mistake.

The second error was trying to hold the plant with just one hand while I scratched a nagging itch behind my ear. That heavy, potted geranium suddenly dropped all the way down to the bottom of the big clay pot, which promptly broke the entire plant off at the base of its branches. *Snap!*

My eyes bugged out of my head. I was now holding a still showy but rootless wonder while the pot full of dirt and roots sat down there in a dark, clay cave.

What would *you* have done, my gardening sister? I did the only thing a girl who's good at cover-ups would do. I quickly filled the clay pot with the most nutrient-rich, expensive black soil I could find, added water, and propped those root-free branches in that pot as if nothing had ever happened. And prayed that Bill would never take a close look at my $39.99 fiasco.

For a day or two, the two plants looked identical—full of red blooms and fragrant leaves. In the same way, we can't always tell by outside appearance alone if someone is connected to Jesus or just hanging around, hoping no one will notice the difference. But that vital difference is undeniable. Before the week was out, the branches without roots wilted, the petals dropped, the leaves drooped.

God, the original gardener, extended a little grace in the direction of my geraniums. After a few branches died off, the main stem grew new roots, and before long new buds began to appear. Teeny-tiny ones, to be sure, but living and rooted nonetheless. *Whew . . .*

> *Lord Jesus, my vine, my source of life,*
> *hold tight to my swaying branches.*
> *I not only want to look alive, Lord,*
> *I want to be alive, ever growing with you.*

THAT'S A KNOW-KNOW

Nevertheless the solid foundation of God stands,
having this seal: "The Lord knows those who are His,"
and, "Let everyone who names the name of Christ
depart from iniquity."

—*2 TIMOTHY 2:19*

As kids, we giggled when adults whispered of someone, "He knew her, in the biblical sense." They usually wiggled their eyebrows when they said it. I wasn't sure what that kind of "knowing" entailed, but it sounded like pretty powerful stuff.

It is. The word *knows* used in 2 Timothy means to have the most intimate understanding of someone. That is how God knows us— intimately, completely, spiritually naked, able to hide nothing from him. I blush at the thought of it.

Sometimes when I'm praying for forgiveness, I begin hesitantly, as if to say, "Lord, you will never believe what I did today." Hold it, Liz. He knows. He knows you, knows your heart, knows your beginning, and knows your ending, and he loves you anyway.

One day I stared such grace in the face. I was barreling along with my cruise control set four miles above the speed limit because someone once told me that was perfectly legal. (Do not try this at home.) It didn't *feel* legal, but it sure did make the trip go faster.

Coming into town, I didn't see the reduced speed limit sign until it was too late. Even as I pressed down the brake pedal, a police car was headed toward me, and I was sure he *knew*. When he turned on his siren and did a quick U-turn behind me, I felt the bottom of my stomach drop to the floorboards. I steered the car over to the gravel shoulder, preparing myself for the inevitable as I braked to a stop.

A dozen excuses were going through my mind while watching in the rearview mirror, knowing any second he would pull up to my rear bumper.

But he didn't. He flew right past me. Didn't slow down, didn't look away, didn't even notice I was there, just kept right on going until he arrived at the accident scene a few hundred yards ahead.

The relief I felt was instantaneous. I'd gotten away with it! No speeding ticket, no lecture, no embarrassment.

Not so fast, Liz. I knew for a fact I was guilty as all get-out; why else would I have pulled over? In truth, I'd just been spared while the one with the power to judge my actions attended to more pressing matters.

In this is grace: God misses nothing, knows everything, and loves us anyway.

Lord, I am humbled with the realization that
you know me better than I know myself.
Thank you for using that knowledge to help me, not to hurt me.

WORDS THAT WOUND, WORDS THAT HEAL

Reckless words pierce like a sword,
but the tongue of the wise brings healing.

—*PROVERBS 12:18 NIV*

Child psychologists agree that our self-image is formed in the first five years of life. Perhaps before this day is out, some memory from childhood will pass through your mind—a look, a word, an activity, something that made a vivid, lifelong impression on you.

If you were to play back those tapes in your head and heart, those self-talk conversations that shape how you feel about yourself, whose voice would be on those tapes, do you suppose? According to two hundred women I surveyed, the remarks we remember most—many of them negative—came from our mothers.

Sorry, Mom. But it's true.

I'm not here to provide fuel for the guilt trip every mother embarks upon when she checks out of the delivery room (Remember, I'm a mother too!). Nor am I anxious to blame your own mother for the way you feel about yourself. Such finger-pointing is nonproductive, even emotionally dangerous.

You're an adult now. The finger of responsibility points in your direction. You can choose to keep repeating those old negative messages, or you can choose how you feel about your body and yourself. You can also choose to mother differently.

Whether my daughter turns out to be model-thin or mama-size, I can guarantee you that within our family circle, Lillian will be loved, hugged, encouraged, praised, and made to feel absolutely beautiful. I know the world will give her a different message, the media will berate her at any size, her friends will always be talking diets, and someday some jerk might tell her he could really love her if she'd "just lose a little weight." I know all that may be in her future.

But here at home she will find a haven, a resting place. Within these walls, her mother—her first role model—is busy living and loving her own full life. A life without apology for my genes or my body. This is the Liz-that-is. Whatever size or shape Lillian turns out to have, it's my fervent prayer that she will accept it, even embrace it as God's gift to her.

This heartfelt message to my daughter is meant for you as well, dear sister:

I love you. God loves you.

And people will love you—the moment you begin to love yourself.

May the words I speak to others offer hope and healing.
May the words I whisper to myself be just as comforting.
May I always speak the truth in love, Lord,
without intentionally inflicting pain, nor absorbing it.
For my daughter's sake. For my sake.
But above all, for your sake and to your glory, Lord.

Now Hear This

And the Word became flesh and dwelt among us,
and we beheld His glory,
the glory as of the only begotten of the Father,
full of grace and truth.

—*John 1:14*

Words matter. They have the power to heal, to hurt, to love, to hate, to change people, to change history.

Then, there's *the* Word, God's Word, the most powerful Word of all.

The earth and everything in it began with the *spoken* Word. "Then God said, 'Let there be light'; and there was light."[10] *Ta-da!* His Word was all it took to create something out of nothing, to form order out of chaos in a universe that was "without form and void," or as Bill loves to say in the Hebrew, *tohu wavohu.* Zip, nada, nothing.

Then in the centuries that followed, God gave us the *written* Word, his holy Scriptures, to teach us everything we need to know about him and, for that matter, about ourselves.

There is much debate raging today about the authenticity of the Bible, about its inerrancy, its inspiration, and so forth. I'm not a theologian and so will never enter into the fray. What I do know is this: The Word of God is so powerful that I believe even a single verse of Scripture can alter a person's life forever. That power must surely come from God, because men have been spilling ink for thousands of years, and most of what's been written is wood, hay, and stubble. Such words couldn't change a lightbulb, let alone a life.

God's Word is dramatically different. For starters, it's timeless: "But the word of our God stands forever."[11] And even though some forty different writers penned the various books of the Bible, the message and themes are seamless and flowing, and echo one another in a way that would have to be called miraculous.

I remember the first sermon from God's Word that I truly *heard*. It was on January 10, 1982, the first time I stepped into a church building as an adult. My dear friends who'd been loving me toward salvation for four months were seated next to me in the pew. When they looked at the text for that day's message, I sensed their shoulders drooping as they whispered, "This will go over like a lead balloon."

The passage that day came from Ephesians: "Wives, submit to your own husbands, as to the Lord."[12] A great teaching, but not the evangelistic, soul-rending message they had prayed for, I fear. As balloons go, this one was indeed floating pretty low. There I sat— a single woman, a woman's libber—thinking, *Yup, this is just the kind of thing I expected at a joint like this: "Get married. Get pregnant. Be a happy little obedient wife."*

God has such a sense of humor. He will do anything to get our attention.

Then the minister read, "Husbands, love your wives, just as Christ also loved the church and gave Himself for her."[13] At that point, I turned to my friend Evelyn and said with a wry smile, "If I ever met a man willing to die for me, I would marry him in a heartbeat!"

"Lizzie," she whispered, "a man has already died for you."

My mind went into overdrive. *Wait a minute. Jesus died for me?* I knew he died for the world, John 3:16 and all that. I knew the basics of Christmas and Easter. But Jesus died for me, personally? Talk about good news!

I listened more intently for the next ten minutes than I've probably ever listened in my life. I knew that very day that *this* was what I'd been looking for all my life—this heavenly love, this gracious forgiveness. Only problem was, I didn't know what to do about it.

In the weeks that followed, I found out exactly what to do —confess my sins, receive his forgiveness, be baptized into new life—and did it with joyous surrender. And the very first thing I did that weekend in February when I gave my heart to the Lord was purchase my own printed copy of his Word. I wanted to see if there were any other verses in there as powerful and life-changing as Ephesians 5:25. (There are.)

He is the spoken Word, he is the written Word, and he is the *living* Word, the fulfillment of that which was both spoken and written. It is yet another of his given titles: "His name is called The Word of God."[14] People may bicker about how the world was created—from Big Bang to extraterrestrials—and they may argue about the inerrancy of the Scriptures, but no one can deny the power of the living Word, Jesus Christ, who can change a person's heart for good.

In the Greek, "word" is *logos*, the perfect Word incarnate, "the Shekinah glory in open manifestation."[15] That's Jesus, all right, the Light of the World and the Word, fulfilled.

Father God, your creation speaks of you,
your holy Scriptures speak of you,
and your Son,
through the power of the Holy Spirit abiding in me,
speaks to my heart about you
all day long.
I can never get enough of your Word!

Suits Me

*And these things we write to you
that your joy may be full.*

—I JOHN 1:4

Fullness of joy is different for all of us, but my joy runneth over when autumn comes and bathing suit season is behind me.

"Bathing Suit Season" is, after all, a loaded term. It doesn't just mean June, July, and August or a week at the Jersey shore. It implies long legs, a golden tan, curves without bulges, a few well-placed freckles, and one very flat stomach.

The Bathing Suit has clout. No other article of clothing has its own season. We don't talk about "Gored Skirt Season" or "Cotton Blouse Season." But the lowly bathing suit, made from half a yard of fabric, carries so much social significance that it has practically replaced the word *summer*.

The problem is, bathing suits have no mercy. They hide nothing. Let's face it, they are little more than printed undergarments. Bras with stripes. Panties with pizzazz. We, who used to run down the hallway shrieking if our older brother saw us in our underwear, happily paraded down a crowded beach later that afternoon, wearing even less.

One-piece swimsuits came in two styles when I was growing up. Either they were made out of armor-thick nylon and elastic (think "foundation") with layers of ruffles and wraps (as if to say, "There's nothing under here but more fabric." Wink. Wink.). Or, they weren't really one-piece suits at all, but rather three-quarter suits, cut out with geometric vengeance, producing circles of sunburn in strange places.

The 1960s also gave us the topless bathing suit. Really, Rudi Gernreich, what were you thinking? Comediennes of the era had a field day. Carol Burnett said she tried a peekaboo bathing suit: People took one peek and said, "Boo." Phyllis Diller described standing on the beach for hours in a topless bathing suit, until she finally got arrested. For loitering. The policeman kept calling her "Mac."

My friend Karla found the perfect way to improve your appearance in a bathing suit: Just raise your arms, pull in your tummy, and lose fifteen years! Of course, that means walking around all day looking like you're about to dive into the pool, but what price vanity?

I remember venturing out in the first bathing suit I'd worn in public in a long time. We were staying at a Colorado Springs hotel—far, far from home. Safe, right? I hid in our room until ten at night, then hustled down to the hotel pool, hoping nobody would be there.

Everybody was there. I took off my ankle-length cover-up and waited for people to start fainting, children to start screaming, the lifeguard to blow his whistle.

Guess what happened?

1. Nobody looked.

2. Nobody cared.

3. Without my glasses, I couldn't see them anyway!

To think of all the joy I missed, hiding on the sidelines all those years.

Don't make the same mistake, sis. So what if you look like you were poured into your bathing suit and forgot to say "when." If it covers the basics and lets you play in the water, dive in!

Lord, my joy did indeed runneth over that night.
Give me the courage to focus on having fun with my family,
instead of focusing on my insecure self.
Let my confidence rest in you,
every season of the year.

Twenty-four/Seven

Have you not known?
Have you not heard?
The everlasting God, the LORD,
The Creator of the ends of the earth,
Neither faints nor is weary.

—Isaiah 40:28

"Nothing lasts forever," the saying goes. Even evergreens really aren't green forever. They're green year-round, but eventually they get struck by lightning, uprooted by the wind, undone by disease, or brought down by a lumberjack.

But God really is everlasting. He will still be around when the universe isn't.

I can, in my own limited way, grasp the idea of forever going forward through time . . . somewhere out there, infinity, forever and ever, amen. But if God is everlasting, he also goes all the way back. Backward not only through time but *before* time, a constraint he created for his purposes and ours.

God is, was, and always will be. And all without a nap.

I am not everlasting. I can't go more than eighteen hours without desperately needing six hours of sleep. When I get tired, both of my "lazy" eyes start wandering . . . could be the left one, could be the right one. All my wedding pictures reveal just how long a day that was: In all the closeup shots, my eyes are looking two different directions. But I'm still smiling!

When my eyes start playing tricks on me, Bill takes one look and says, "Time for bed." The last thing he wants is a weary, whiny woman on his hands.

Bill, on the other hand, gets this bleary, glazed look. Both his eyes are pointed straight ahead but out of focus. The lights are on, but nobody's home. "Sleepy time," I say softly, and off to bed he goes. Suffice to say, we are not everlasting.

How comforting to know that while we sleep, God does not. We are temporal, he is eternal. To him, one day is like a thousand, and in all of them, he's on the throne and wide awake.

Lord, knowing that you are the very definition of eternity
makes me want to live there.
Let me rest in the knowledge that
"even from everlasting to everlasting,
You are God."[16]

BUILDING UP
YOUR MATE

So encourage each other and build each other up,
just as you are already doing.

—1 THESSALONIANS 5:11 NLT

Bill and I once wrote an article together called "Seven Ways to Tear Down (or Build Up) Your Mate." WARNING: Do not try this at home.

"Bill," I began, as my hands hovered over the computer keyboard, "why don't you come up with a list of various ways we unintentionally tear each other down? I'll do the same, and then we'll compare notes."

"Fine," he said, dropping into the chair beside my desk. "I've been thinking about the time we were driving to my parents' house."

"Nah, that'll never work," I said with conviction, my eyes still glued to the computer screen. "Too negative."

"No, I mean that time over Christmas when the kids . . ."

"I remember what happened!" I said, exasperated. "Your mom made some comment about Matthew's grades . . ."

"Not that time, Liz."

"And then I said she didn't understand the situation, and then she said . . ."

"Please let me finish!" Bill's volume control had moved up three full notches.

"Finish what?" I asked innocently.

He jumped to his feet. "That will be the first thing on my list!"

"What list?" My dancing fingers paused over the keyboard.

"The list of the seven ways we tear each other down. 'Not letting me finish a sentence' will be number one!"

"Do I do that?" My expression was pure Shirley Temple.

"Oh, brother!" Bill rolled his eyes toward the heavens. "Honey, sometimes you're so sure of what I'm going to say next, you say it for me, even if that's not the direction I'm headed at all."

"Oh, sorry." Sheepish grin. "I'll try to do better. Now . . . what were you saying?"

I recently stumbled upon a horrible verse in Proverbs: "Better to dwell in a corner of a housetop, / Than in a house shared with a contentious woman." Even worse, that very same verse shows up twice—in Proverbs 21:9 and Proverbs 25:24! *Lord, is that a hint?* King Solomon, who wrote down most of the book of Proverbs, obviously had an ax to grind. Or else he was talking about two different wives (after all, he had several hundred).

Bill and I have learned (the hard way) that the best method for affirming one another is to *listen:* eyes open, ears open, heart open, mouth shut. Occasional nodding helps too.

Bill deserves my full attention, Lord.
And my full support.
Help me build him up,
not tear him down.
Help me keep my whining to a minimum
and my listening to a maximum.
My husband is the nicest earthly gift
you've ever given me, Lord.
May my gratitude show in how often I encourage him,
day in and day out.

HE'S THE ONE

For God, who said, "Light shall shine out of darkness,"
is the One who has shone in our hearts to give the Light of
the knowledge of the glory of God in the face of Christ.

—2 CORINTHIANS 4:6 NASB

On the day I was baptized, I wanted to wear a white dress. Corny, maybe, but I saw it as a symbol of purity, of being made new. This great idea had one fatal flaw: You can't find a white dress in February unless it's made out of wool, which makes me itch like the dickens.

So I settled on another symbolic purchase—a small, gold cross, which at $7.99 was also a lot *cheaper* than a white dress. I slipped it on a plain, gold necklace that already had a charm attached—a gold outline of a heart—and stood back to admire my new jewelry in the mirror.

The two charms looked great hanging there, side by side, the heart and the cross. However, within minutes they became hopelessly tangled together as the cross got lodged sideways in the open heart. I'd no sooner get them carefully separated than they would get stuck together again.

The message here is not subtle: Jesus comes into your life for good.

When Jesus entered my heart with his blazing light of truth, it's a wonder he stayed at all. I shudder to think of the filthy debris he found there, the sad remains of dozens of painful relationships with men I'd invited into my heart to stay but who'd only stopped by for a short visit.

Only the One who loves us could see beauty among such ruin; only the One who cares for us would be willing to roll up his spiritual sleeves and discard the dark, dank debris in order to make room for his shining light.

Only Jesus is the One. He's called the chosen One, the expected One, the holy One, the living One, the mighty One, the righteous One . . . he's the One!

Lord, with you, One is a whole number.
Thank you for being the right One for me.
And not for me alone, but for everyone.

From Beginning to End

I am the Alpha and the Omega,
the Beginning and the End,
the First and the Last.

—Revelation 22:13

Where did *you* land in the lineup for graduation—"A" for Adams, "Z" for Zimmerman, or somewhere in the middle?

Growing up with a last name that began with "A" meant I always stood at the head of the line, always sat in the front of the classroom, always had to recite my Latin translation first, always had all eyes on me when I tried to do a cartwheel in gym class. (By the time we got to Debbie Royer's cartwheel, everyone's attention had switched to boys and homework—humph!)

That's the thing about going first: You're expected to set the pace for everyone else, to light the path, take the heat, work out all the kinks, show everyone that it can be done, and teach them how to do it as well. Ask any firstborn child, and he or she will tell you exactly how much pressure goes along with going first.

On the other hand, when we lined up by height for Glee Club, tall Lizzie had to go last and take my place in the back row with the basses. As the last one in line, my primary responsibility was to make sure everyone stayed in place and didn't head off in the wrong direction. Plus, the last person had to turn the lights out, close the door of the rehearsal room, and make certain no one fell off the risers onstage. (Remember how hot it got in those robes?)

That's the thing about going last. You are expected to follow up, clean up, and check up on everything, plus display endless patience and attention to detail. It's just as much responsibility as going first, but few people realize how much behind-the-scenes work there is.

Jesus, who is both First and Last, understands.

He is the Alpha, the Beginning, the Firstfruits of the kingdom. He's your spiritual older brother who not only lights your path but also *is* the path. By letting him go first as your Leader, you know you're headed in the right direction and can follow his example with confidence.

You can also take comfort in knowing he goes last. No need to look back, or start worrying, or do a follow-up call. When Jesus said, "It is finished!"[17] that settled it. Calvary was once for all. He walked to the cross alone as the Alpha, the Only Begotten, the First, and rose triumphantly as the Omega, the End, the Last.

These days, I am neither first nor last. Since my name is now "Mrs. Higgs," I fall somewhere in the middle of the alphabetical roll call. I've decided that being in the middle is the safest, surest place to be. With my fearless Leader fore and aft, I can finally relax and know someone else is in charge.

Lord, I'm so grateful that you go before me and behind me.
When I lose sight of my destination, help me to simply focus
on your strong back and keep walking.

WHEN YOU STUMBLE

When pride comes, then comes shame;
But with the humble is wisdom.

—PROVERBS 11:2

Perhaps if you join me on a brief journey from pride to shame to wisdom, you can skip the first two painful steps and go straight to being wise.

February 1993. Newport Beach, California. The National Speakers Association, my peer group of the hour, was gathered for their winter educational workshop, and I was invited to be their Saturday evening speaker.

Big honor. Big blessing. Big ego alert.

I should have seen disaster on the horizon, even from two thousand miles away.

For starters, I had spoken in Columbus, Ohio, that same morning and so had to fly out at 1:00 P.M. for the West Coast, hoping and praying my flight would land on time. I arrived at 5:00 with the main event just two hours away and my nerves stretched to the limit. Toss in a three-hour time change and a little jet lag for good measure, and you get some sense of my level of energy at this point.

It gets worse.

The huge meal (for some, with wine) took a l-o-n-g time to serve. Beef—heavy, sleep-inducing beef—was on the menu. And baked potatoes. And cheesecake. *Zzzzzzz*. A thirty-minute slide presentation of fine art preceded my program. Oh, that perked people right up.

It was late—well after 9:00—when I finally stepped on the stage. By my body clock, it felt like midnight, as it did for many attendees. The room was dimly lit, with large mirrored posts blocking both my view and theirs. Everywhere I looked, I saw Liz, and Liz looked nervous. The five hundred attendees were, for the most part, speakers, fully capable of doing what I was about to do and curious to see why I was invited to do so instead of them.

You get the picture. Pressure City.

If it sounds as though I'm making excuses, you're absolutely right. Even though I'd prayed, prepared, and practiced, I laid an egg in Newport Beach. It was the longest hour I've ever spent on the platform. I tried all my funniest stories, to no avail. The few times folks did laugh, it had a strained, let's-help-her-out quality.

There is no death like dying on the platform.

I could feel my hair turning gray as I spoke. Everywhere I looked, I saw mirrored images of myself. Bombing. Comedian David Brenner says when you do humor, you can't get good without bombing. But, David, did it have to be that night?!

When I finally finished, the audience leaped to their feet—and ran out the door. I'd hoped for a standing ovation; this was more like a running ovation.

Days later I was licking my wounds at home in Louisville, certain that I'd never show my face at another association gathering again, when the unthinkable happened. The program chair for the big National Convention in Washington, D.C., called and asked me to do a program to kick off the whole event.

I was stunned to silence. The committee members must not have been in Newport Beach! The obvious solution was to say no thanks, but it's such an honor to be asked that speakers almost never refuse.

My heart was in my throat (or was it my shoes?). I needed help and fast, so I faxed a dear friend of mine, Rosita Perez, a consummate pro in the speaking business and the one who'd introduced me that fateful night. "Rosita," I wrote, "how am I going to get back up on the platform? You were in Newport Beach; you saw me bomb. What am I going to do?"

She faxed me back. "Liz, you did not bomb; it just wasn't magic." (Rosita is a motivational speaker. They say things like that.) Her fax went on, "Let me ask you something: Do you like Dustin Hoffman?"

Dustin Hoffman?! Was he in Newport Beach?

Her fax continued. "He's a brilliant actor, yes? Award-winning, an incredible talent, a Hollywood legend, yes?"

Yes, yes.

"Did you see him in *Ishtar*?"

Oh, I'd seen *Ishtar*, back when I reviewed movies for a local radio station. I declared it the single worst movie I'd ever paid money to see. That distinction still stands. Forty million dollars, Warren Beatty, Dustin Hoffman—a bomb. A big bomb. In fact, one of my favorite cartoons from *The Far Side* showed a video store in Hades, with nothing on the shelves but *Ishtar, Ishtar, Ishtar* . . .

"So, Liz," her fax concluded, "if Dustin Hoffman can survive an

Ishtar in his career and come back and win an Oscar for Best Actor in *Rain Man*, can't you get back up on that platform?"

Rosita had me there. The more I thought about it, the more excited I got. Yes, I would get back up on that horse. If I fell off again, at least I knew I could survive.

Inspired by her words, I sat down at my computer and created a graphic reminder of my meaningful discovery:

ISHTAR HAPPENS

It happened to Dustin, it happened to me in Newport Beach, and if/when it happens to you, now you'll be ready. There's a Japanese proverb that says, "When you stumble, don't get up empty-handed." Indeed, if you stand up with your head full of wisdom and your heart full of laughter, who knows what might happen?

Lord, you knew that night would be an Ishtar-size disaster.
Forgive the pride that put me on that platform in the first place.
I rest in knowing that, despite my serious stumbling,
you were with me through it all.

Rocky Mountain High

*Praise the L*ORD*, call upon His name;*
Declare His deeds among the peoples,
Make mention that His name is exalted.

—I*SAIAH* 12:4

On a summer vacation in the Rocky Mountain National Park, we picked the foggiest day on record to drive the scenic Trail Ridge Road, the highest completely paved road in the United States. We just *knew* there were mountains out there somewhere, but we sure couldn't see them. We'd drive past signs for scenic overlooks, and the only thing to look over was more fog.

We were quite certain we were heading up the mountain, though, because there was snow piled along the side of the road six to eight feet high . . . in June! When we hit the highest point on the road, 12,123 feet above sea level, we jumped out to sample the clean air and found the air is indeed rare up there. Don't climb any rocks, or you might pass out!

That night we crawled into bed in our log cabin at Longs Peak Conference Center, surrounded by the damp, chilly mist, never dreaming what we'd find when we woke up the next morning. The sun was peeking around the window shade, so I reached out a sleepy hand to raise the shade and almost fainted.

We had a mountain in our backyard—a big mountain! Longs Peak is 14,255 feet high. The blinding sun made every snow-covered inch look like it might fall on us at any moment. "The mountain is out!" the kids squealed.

What a humbling experience. Although I knew intellectually that the mountain was there—after all, it was on the map and probably hadn't moved lately—because I couldn't see it with my own eyes, it was not a reality to me.

During those twenty-seven years I spent apart from Christ, he was just like that mountain. Enormous, immovable, right there, right next to me, but I was in a fog and saw him not. Then one day the fog cleared and *boom!* Look up, Liz. The exalted One is here. In truth, he was there all along, but now I had eyes to see him.

Soon it was time to say good-bye to our backyard mountain. Driving down Route 7 toward Denver, I couldn't take my eyes off the snowcapped peaks in my rearview mirror. So majestic, so solid, so timeless, so *big*. And to think that our God created them. These are mere hills to him. Yet when he looks down on his creation, it's not his mountains that he can't take his eyes off of . . . it's us.

Lord, when I consider the works of your hands,
the mountains and the hills that you have ordained,
I am humbled to know
that you think of me at all.

Hair Today, Gone Tomorrow

But the very hairs of your head are all numbered.

—Matthew 10:30

When you rise this morning and the light in your bathroom shines on the tub, might you find a stray hair or two sliding down the drain with the suds? *Uh-uh.*

Two thousand years ago, the apostle Paul declared that "not a hair will fall from the head of any of you."[18] That may be true for those faithful few, but for the less lucky among us, it's curtains for our curly locks.

I'm not sure when the first hair slithered out of my scalp, quietly and without fanfare, but, like Hansel and Gretel, that first silken strand left behind a faint trail of shampoo crumbs for others to follow. Soon I discovered that in certain overhead lighting situations—no, it's not possible!—I could see my scalp peeking through my bottle-blond tresses.

I've borrowed a page from the fellas on this one and am moving my part farther and farther to the left so I have plenty to comb over my sparse spot. At least I'm not combing it all into one big swirl on top! Bless their hearts, some men get out of the pool with one eight-foot hair hanging down and have to tuck it in their bathing trunks to keep from tripping over it.

When I mention my thinning hair during my presentations, two things are guaranteed to happen: (1) Women in the audience will start squinting and staring very pointedly at my scalp, then turn to one another, nodding: *She's right;* and (2) Some well-meaning soul will slip a piece of paper into my hand with the name of a shampoo meant for horses (to which I say, "Neigh!") or the telephone number of her own salon with the notation, "We can help you."

Let me say this as gently as possible: My fine hair is . . . fine. If the Lord, who created the universe and rules it as well, can't answer my prayers on this one, then I'll do what I always do when I stumble over an immovable object: Laugh!

As Georgia Ann has discovered, the top of your head isn't the only place where the hairs come tumbling down: "One evening as I was gazing at my reflection in the bathroom mirror, I got my old eyelash curler out of the cabinet, positioned it on my eyelid, and burst into laughter. There were no eyelashes long and strong enough to curl!"

Eyelashes can be bought, eyebrows can be drawn on (do try to avoid the perpetually "surprised" look), hats can be worn on cool days (I have six), and wigs are a distinct possibility. In another lifetime (that is, twenty-some years ago), I worked at a wig shop. Not a fancy one, the kind at the mall with the $12.95 Eva Gabor specials. In those days, the state of the art for wigs was pretty dismal. Now you can find wigs that are so real-looking, if you don't know—you don't know.

I complimented a woman once who had a fabulous flip with bangs. She smiled broadly and said, "Thanks, Liz. I just had chemo, so instead of wearing a scarf I bought a wig. Sure wish mine would grow out this color!"

Don't you love her positive outlook? She knows there's more to life than thick hair.

Maybe, instead of joining The Hair(less) Club for Women, I'll make the switch from bottled hair to bought hair. Only your wig seller knows for sure.

Since "the very hairs of your head are all numbered," even those of us who never got above a C in algebra will be able to count every blessed one of ours. We'll also have less hair to wash, dry, style, comb, detangle, and color. Now if our salons would only give us a hairs-per-capita discount . . .

> Lord Jesus, thanks for counting my hairs
> so I don't have to.
> In truth, no matter how much I lift and comb it,
> my hair has no lofty thoughts of you.
> It's the mind beneath my scalp,
> meditating on you and your Word,
> that matters most to you,
> not the strands of hair above it,
> however thick or thin they might be.

Pain Management

There shall be no more pain,
for the former things have passed away.

—*Revelation 21:4b*

Have you awakened this morning with stiff joints or a pain in the neck or a sore back, babe?

Here's a story that might take your mind off things, if only for a moment.

I had a speech in Louisville one chilly Saturday in January. After a whole week of snow, sleet, rain, snow, sleet, rain, the parking lots in town were covered with *snirt*—snow and dirt. Underneath the snirt was *sneet*—snow and sleet—and underneath the sneet was a thin layer of ice, which you couldn't see for all the snirt and the sneet.

In typical Lizzie fashion, I arrived late, sliding into the parking lot mere minutes before the opening remarks. I leaped out of the car and grabbed my purse, along with a big stack of handouts. I didn't get two feet before I hit a patch of ice hiding underneath the snirt and the sneet and went sailing across the ice, first in vertical, then horizontal, fashion.

Since I never remember to zip my purse, the contents went flying everywhere, soon followed by my handouts. (Paper and snirt are a bad combination.) Lying there on the ice, stunned senseless, I contemplated my best options for standing up.

Across the snowy parking lot floated the voice of an angel wearing the uniform of a maintenance man. "Are you okay?" he called across the empty spaces.

"No, I'm not!" I moaned, assessing the damage while he made his way toward me.

I'd not torn my dress or ruined my hose, and I had only a few spots of snirt and sneet to brush away. So far so good. But when the kind man helped me get up (I'll spare you the horrid details), I discovered that everything hurt down the left side, from shoulder to ankle. I'd hit that snirty pavement harder than I realized and was now in severe pain, feeling bruises already in the making.

I had no choice. I had to speak. With my angelic hero's guidance, I carefully hobbled across the snirt, brushed myself off, and headed for the front of the auditorium, wincing with every step.

"So glad to be with you this morning!" My lips were smiling, but the rest of my body gave a whole different message. I was listing to the left and gesturing with my right hand as the left one clutched the lectern for support. How in the world would I make it through an hour-long presentation?

An amazing thing happened. As if on cue, the audience started laughing, which made me laugh. They laughed, I laughed, they laughed, I laughed. Sixty minutes later, nothing hurt! Thanks to the adrenaline flow that begins when a performer hits the stage, and an endorphin or two that made an appearance, I felt no pain whatsoever. At the end of my speech, I was so excited, I ran out in the parking lot and almost fell down again.

When I got home, I exclaimed, "Bill! I thought I hurt myself, but I didn't!"

Right.

An hour later the adrenaline wore off, and the aches and pains came back. But I believe the laughter bought me some time from the pain.

Josh Billings said, "One of the hardest things for any man to do is to fall down on the ice and then get up and praise the Lord." Amen to that, brother! But if you can get up and *laugh*, then praising the Lord will soon follow.

Lord Jesus, thank you for easing my pain,
if only for an hour,
and allowing me to laugh
rather than moan and groan.
It's a choice, isn't it, Lord?
To laugh, even in difficult circumstances.
To mend our funny bone first,
knowing the rest of our bones will follow.
Bless you for being a Great Physician who heals
with laughter.

Living Abundantly

Even to your old age, I am He,
And even to gray hairs I will carry you!

—Isaiah 46:4a

The French novelist Colette declared, "What a wonderful life I've had! I only wish I'd realized it sooner." Maybe today is your day to realize that, at any age, it's never too late to have a wonderful life.

Fifty is fabulous, according to the women I've heard from who call it "life-affirming," "a relief," and "like waking up." Judith shares: "Fifty was spent alone. I considered it a Rite of Passage. I had time to reflect on the past and look ahead with a plan and direction."

Sixty looks super when seen through the eyes of a woman who has been there. Kay says you have "enough experiences under your belt to take life as it comes, with the assurance that in both the good and bad times, happy and sad times, God is there bringing meaning and purpose in all times."

Seventy sounds stupendous, according to Flo, who remembers, "My seventieth birthday was my first birthday party in sixty-three years and by far the better of the two. (So few showed up at my seventh birthday, due to a more affluent party on the same day, same street!) On my seventieth, all my friends came to a potluck party given by my youngest daughter. The entire theme was 'Aged to Perfection.'"

Eighty is awesome, at least when you're Elsie: "If you survive until you are eighty, everybody is surprised that you're still alive. They treat you with respect for having lived so long. (Actually, they seem surprised that you can walk and talk sensibly!) People forgive you for everything. If you ask me, life begins at eighty."

I rode on a hotel shuttle bus in Montana a few years ago with a woman who was delighted to tell me she was eighty. "What brought you to Great Falls?" I asked her, just making conversation.

She'd spent a week at a dude ranch, that's what. That was after spending four days in Portland, Oregon, riding a big paddle wheeler up the Willamette River. Alone.

"What prompted you to do that?" I asked her, amazed.

"My friends just got back from there and said it was not to be missed," she explained. Apparently, this woman missed nothing.

"I already had a trip to California lined up but managed to squeeze in Portland. I've been on the road for a month."

I was speechless. At half her age, it's all I can do to manage four days on the road.

She continued, "I just hope my ankle won't bother me."

I looked down to examine her bundled foot. "My goodness. What happened?" I asked, genuinely concerned for this spry adventurer.

"Oh, I twisted it horseback riding yesterday." With that, she eased out the door of the shuttle and headed toward the terminal calling out to no one in particular, "Can you tell me where I might find Alaska Airlines?"

My hero.

These women encourage me, Lord!
To know that life is far from over
at fifty, or sixty, or seventy, or beyond.
To see the possibilities and know that you will be with me
through every one of them.
Give me a ticket for an airplane, Lord.
I'm ready when you are.
And you are always ready

Practically Perfect

*. . . by one sacrifice he has made perfect forever
those who are being made holy.*

—*Hebrews 10:14* NIV

Feeling perfect this morning, dear heart? Or does perfection seem like a distant carrot, beyond your grasp?

You'll remember our childhood heroine Mary Poppins, who stretched a tape measure up to the tippy-top of her flower-bedecked hat and announced she was "practically perfect in every way."

Well, jolly good for you, I remember thinking as a child. I wasn't perfect in any way at all. The mirror told me I was barely so-so, my grades were less than 4.0, my friends were fickle, my parents were hard to please.

Perfect? Not this girl. Especially if a tape measure was involved. Very scary.

Fast-forward to 1982 and my close encounter of the life-changing kind with the Lord. "Be perfect as I am perfect," he said.[19]

"But, Lord," I groaned, "I've been trying to be perfect all my life, and look what a mess I've made of things. A perfectionist who isn't perfect—what a sorry excuse for womanhood *that* is!"

Four years of high school Latin are (finally) about to be put to use:

"Perfect" is derived from the Latin verb *perficere*, which means "to finish." Something is "perfect" when it is made complete in every way. We are promised in God's Word that "He who has begun a good work in you will complete it until the day of Jesus Christ."[20]

Complete. Finished. All done. Nothing more is needed. Perfect in every way.

So, when we're completely his, we're made perfect, too.

Years ago, the first intelligible words out of our daughter Lillian's mouth were—appropriately—"Ta-da!" Her daddy had just helped her do her first somersault, and she threw her toddler arms up in a victory salute. The look on her face was pure joy at the completion of her gymnastic feat: "Ta-da!"

I encourage women to try the same thing. (No, no, not the somersault!) Simply stand in front of a mirror—fully dressed, of course—stretch out your arms with joy and say it like you mean it: "Ta-da!"

That's what God says when he looks upon you, dear one. "Ta-da! I did it! She's perfect, she's finished, and she's all mine." You are gorgeous to God simply because you're covered in the blood of his Son. Neither a perfect fool nor a perfect stranger, you are practically, spiritually perfect in every way because of his perfection . . . not your own.

What freedom there is in that!

Lord, help me stop shying away from
mirrors and tape measures,
and instead see them as joy-filled reminders
that I stand tall
in your perfect grace.

GLAD RAP

Be glad in the LORD and rejoice, you righteous;
And shout for joy, all you upright in heart!

—PSALM 32:11

While your coffee is brewing this morning, see if you have hiding in your kitchen cabinet a handy box of clear polyethylene, better known as GLAD Cling Wrap. Good stuff, this. The box proudly proclaims all the benefits of being GLAD:

GLAD Is Easy to Handle. I couldn't agree more. Give me a glad person to work with any day. Not overly sensitive, not demanding, just glad to be alive and easy to get along with.

GLAD Keeps Things Fresh. Nothing like a new perspective to make life interesting. People who are glad are fun to be around—refreshing, in fact.

GLAD Is Transparent. And that's just what it takes to let Christ shine through us: a see-through, crystal-clear life. "You is what you is," and we're glad, too.

GLAD Is Great for All Uses. Don't you love those flexible folks who are glad to be useful and can do anything you ask without complaining?

GLAD Is Tough and Durable. Just because you're flexible and transparent doesn't mean you're not tough. Even when your life is turned upside down, stuff doesn't fall out when you're covered with gladness!

GLAD Forms a Tight Seal. Tighter than the love of earthly family is the love between the Lord and his beloved children. "Set me as a seal upon your heart."[21]

You see, glad is a handy thing to be in God's kingdom. Those who are glad are able to rejoice and shout for joy with an *exclamation point!* And as a writer who loves that form of punctuation, I get excited when it shows up in Scripture. We're talking big happy here. Be ye glad!

Lord, I know being glad is
a decision of my will,
not merely an expression of my emotions.
Help me be easy to handle and ever refreshing,
always tough and eternally durable.
Shine through my see-through self,
and seal me with your love.
How glad I am to be
yours!

Word for Word

The grass withers, the flower fades,
But the word of our God stands forever.

—Isaiah 40:8

The most important words in this book are God's words: the holy Scriptures.

His Word tells us the truth, consistently and without wavering, untouched by the whims of emotion and circumstance. Whether you are a brand-new Christian, a longtime believer, a silver-haired saint, or a just-coming-back-to-the-fold prodigal daughter, you can count on God's Word to give you a true picture of his boundless love for you.

Don't be distracted or deceived by how you feel about yourself, what you see when you look in the mirror, how much money you have in the bank, what kind of car you drive or the house you live in, whether you are married or not, whether you're highly educated or just squeaked by in school.

These things are temporal. God's promises are eternal.

What matters is that we're following the leading of his Word, that we're on the right path, eager to move forward, willing to be transformed into his image, day by day, moment by moment.

The Word of God is a mirror that changes us each time we look into it. Just one glance might make a few alterations, but a true metamorphosis comes from longer gazes, drinking in all the details.

Here is what God has said to me:

Liz, if you can spend fifteen minutes a day getting your hair and makeup in place while staring in a mirror that will never change you permanently, then you can find fifteen minutes to look into my Word, a mirror that will change you, inside and out, and make you even more beautiful to me!

Does the Lord deserve more time than fifteen minutes? Of course.

But it's a start, sis. It's a beginning. That's why we're here this morning, yes?

Thank you, Lord Jesus,
for your unchangeable Word.
It comforts and admonishes me.
It makes me smile and it makes me cry.
It reminds me of your holiness and my wretchedness.
It showers me with grace and gives me hope.
In a shaky world, your Word is a solid foundation.
Thank you for the gift of Truth
shining across its sacred pages.

'Til Death (or High Water) Do Us Part

Bear with each other and forgive whatever grievances
you may have against one another.
Forgive as the Lord forgave you.
And over all these virtues put on love,
which binds them all together in perfect unity.

—Colossians 3:13–14 NIV

True Love knows no age boundaries, according to Loretta from Kentucky. Her daughter came home from her first week at kindergarten and announced that she was in love with a boy in her class. Her father said, "Don't you think you're a little young?" She replied brightly, "No, Daddy. He's five and I'm five!"

Bill and I were nearly three decades older when True Love came calling. It was Valentine's Day, and we were exactly one month away from our wedding day. On that cold, wintry holiday evening, Bill had driven seventy miles in a blinding snowstorm to present me with my favorite flowers: red tulips. No doubt about it, it was True Love.

Not to be outdone, I had spent the afternoon slicing apples into tiny slivers and rolling out a from-scratch crust to make a dessert fit for my prince: French apple pie. Classical music, candlelight on the coffee table. *Isn't marriage going to be bliss?* I thought as we cuddled on the couch and watched the falling snow.

Fast-forward to another Valentine's Day—nine years, several pounds, and two children later. A bigger mortgage, much more laundry, two cars brimming with fast-food bags and Sunday school take-home papers. No tulips. No apple pie. No snow. No doubt about it, it was . . . True Love.

Not Hollywood love. Not love at first sight. Not convenient love. Not conditional love. The Real Thing. Love based on commitment, on acceptance, on day-in and day-out, and never-mind-the-seven-year-itch perseverance. It's not always exciting. In fact, It would make a dull soap opera script. Barbara Bush once said, "I married the first man I ever kissed. When I tell my children that, they just about throw up." That's True Love for you. Love for the long haul, whenever it begins.

As is the custom now, Bill and I had our wedding videotaped. It's a good thing because the entire day was one happy blur. I was so proud of us, both sentimental fools, for not crying a drop. We sang, we laughed, and the guests almost clapped when we turned to be introduced: "Ladies and gentlemen, Dr. and Mrs. William Higgs!" It was an evening of transcendent joy.

But now, when I watch the videotape, I cry like a baby. "Look how young we were!" I sniff. The tears really start to roll when we begin repeating our vows. *What were we saying?* I think, shaking my head in disbelief.

We were saying we would do several outrageously difficult

things for the rest of our natural lives, stuff that would be hard to do for a week unless it were really True Love.

Some people say, "As long as we both shall love," but Bill and I decided to go for a life term and stuck with the traditional, "'til death do us part." Until then, handsome man, I'm all yours. And *you*—thank the Lord—are all mine.

When we said those vows in your presence, Lord,
so many years ago,
we had no idea what we were getting ourselves into.
But you knew.
Thank you for defining True Love for us:
your love.
Even when "death do us part,"
we will be in your presence
together.
Oh, happy day!

NICE HOUSE

For our citizenship is in heaven, from which we also
eagerly wait for the Savior, the Lord Jesus Christ.

—PHILIPPIANS 3:20

If you meet someone new today, see if you find yourself doing what many of us instinctively do: Soon after we ask, "What's your name?" and "Where do you work?" we'll get around to inquiring, "What part of town do you live in?"

An odd question. Are we planning to drop off a casserole anytime soon? Deliver the dry cleaning, maybe? Some of it is natural curiosity, but, to be honest, some of it is just being nosy.

Like it or not, we often judge one another by the house we live in. Tell someone the name of your street or subdivision, and listen for their "Oh" response:

"Oh??"   (Poor thing, what a shame she can't do better.)

"Ohh . . ."   (Not bad for a starter home. Maybe she'll move up soon.)

"Ooooh!"   (How can she possibly afford that? Think of the mortgage payments!)

Rather foolish, considering the buildings we call home today are just a temporary residence and of no eternal significance. Even if it's a seven-thousand-square-foot executive home with a Jacuzzi in every bedroom, it's a pup tent compared to the permanent home that awaits you in heaven: walls of jasper, sapphire, and emerald; streets of pure gold; gates of pearl; and, best of all, Jesus your Host, awaiting your arrival.

The next time you fill out a magazine subscription card with your street, city, state, and zip code, and it asks, "Is this a permanent address?" be honest and check off *No.*

For me, Louisville is where I serve, but heaven is where I plan to spend eternity. Won't moving day be fun?

Lord, why do I get so wrapped up in
buying, selling,
designing, and decorating
my earthly home,
when it's my heavenly address
that matters most?
Help me be grateful for the roof over my head,
however humble it may be.
Keep my eyes fixed on the mansion
you're even now preparing for me.

CONFIDENTIALLY SPEAKING

In the fear of the LORD there is strong confidence,
And His children will have a place of refuge.

—PROVERBS 14:26

Come with me to Colorado Springs, where I'd just experienced a true "Rocky Mountain high" with a whole roomful of wonderful, worshipful women. I stepped off the stage and was weaving through the crowd toward the book table when I was stopped by an enthusiastic attendee with a big grin on her face.

"Liz," she began, clasping my hand in hers, "when I saw you walk out on the platform, I said to my friend, 'Hey, there's hope for us all!'"

I laughed out loud, realizing she meant no offense—and also knowing how very right she was. If you've met me or seen my photo, you'd probably agree that in no way would I ever fit the standard description of a "platform personality." I'm not the right size, the right shape, or the right age for stardom. I'm not highly degreed (my bachelor of arts in English was earned after eighteen years and three colleges), and my favorite credentials are M.O.M.

Sure, I've done several hundred media interviews over the years, but let's be truthful: "Liz Curtis Higgs" is hardly a household name.

The proof is in my mailbox. I get letters addressed to Liza or Lisa, Curtin or Carter, not to mention Higgins, Hicks, Haigs, Huggs, and—too close for comfort—Hoggs. My favorite bloopers were the letter addressed to Liz Taylor Higgs and the check I received made payable to that famous mystery writer Liz Higgins Clark!

So you see, the woman in Colorado Springs was correct: There *is* hope for us all. If Liz—with an overly abundant body, chemically dependent hair, and noncelebrity status—can muster enough confidence to speak for the Lord, then rest assured that God can use you right now, "as is," if you'll just let him.

Some people call it "self-confidence," but I know better. Jesus warned us that unless we're connected to him we can't do anything. At this point in my journey of faith, I've discovered that *real* confidence comes from the Lord. Specifically, it comes from knowing absolutely that these two statements are the Truth:

1. *Jesus is the Master of the Universe and worthy of our trust.*

2. *We who call him Lord are his children and worthy of his love.*

No wonder they call it good news!

When my confidence wavers, Lord Jesus,
help me be confident in you.
When I am weak, remind me
that you are
more than strong enough
for both of us.

TOO GOOD TO BE TRUE

An excellent wife, who can find?

—PROVERBS 31:10A NASB

Ask eight hundred women to define "the perfect wife," and you'll get eight hundred answers with one conclusion: She doesn't exist. Gloria described her as "having no flaws, making no mistakes. There is no such thing!" Susan is sure she is a "nonmortal being that lives in our imagination, setting a standard that is not humanly possible to achieve." Then there's Dauna, who writes, "The definition of a perfect wife eludes me, but I think every woman needs one!"

So, what's the Lord trying to tell us in Proverbs 31 about a man looking for an "excellent" wife? The list of qualities and skills expected from this wonder woman is exhausting: self-confident, trustworthy, good with money, devoted to her husband, creative, a gourmet cook, a land developer, strong in character and muscle, sensitive and discerning, hardworking, generous, an expert seamstress, a terrific home decorator, well dressed, self-employed, quick to laugh, never idle, loved by her children, praised by her husband, faithful to God, and well respected by the entire community. In fact, "she was voted B.C. 1015's top of the top ten. The honor came complete with halo and wings."[22]

"Give me a break!" you say? Happy to. Jill Briscoe calls this perfect woman of Proverbs 31 a "Statue of Liberty,"[23] meaning she's a symbol, larger than life—*not* a real, living, breathing woman who once roamed the earth. Even scholars assure us, "This lady's standard is not implied to be in reach of all," but instead she's "a universal type of woman."[24]

You mean Proverbs 31:10–31 is meant to be a list of the best qualities of womanhood—not the attributes of one woman? Girlfriend, am I ever relieved! She's not so much a role model as role *models*.

When I surveyed eight hundred women to find out "Who serves as a role model for you . . . and why?" nearly 10 percent specifically wrote "none" in all three categories—professional life, family life, spiritual life. It isn't that we don't want role models—we are desperate for them. But everywhere we look are people who disappoint us, people who keep lowering their own standards, people who teach us more about how *not* to act than how to act.

That's why the many excellent women described in Proverbs 31 are so appealing to me. They have withstood the test of time, wrinkle free. Their truths are eternal; their wisdom spans the ages. These women aren't perfect, but they *are* excellent. And at least one of them can laugh at the days to come!

Father God, sometimes this Proverbs 31 list wears me out.
After I have done my best to live up to such virtues,
let me embrace grace rather than perfection
and extend grace rather than judgment to my sisters.
When it comes to excellence, Lord,
you are first on the list.

LOOKING FOR LAUGHTER

He who is of a merry heart has a continual feast.

—PROVERBS 15:15B

Your assignment for today, beloved?

Be on the lookout for laughter.

We were hunting for moose—not amusement—when we went north to Alaska a decade ago, preschoolers in tow. This moose-hunting trip was not the kind of hunting with guns and trophies and such. This was an "Oh, look! A moose!" sort of venture as we traveled the highway between Anchorage and Talkeetna.

We kept our eyes glued to the woods along the roadside, slowing down at the moosiest-looking spots, certain we'd spy one any minute. Sadly, the first day came and went without a single sighting.

Dinner that evening at the Klondike Café featured salmon (what else?) for Mom and Dad, burgers for the kids. I suggested they try the reindeer meat, but four-year-old Lillian's eyes teared up at the very idea of serving Donner and Blitzen with ketchup. When Bill spotted moose meat on the menu, Matthew just rolled his eyes. "Dad, we'd like to see a *live* moose, not a cooked one."

By our last day, we were in major moose-hunting mode, desperate to see one of Alaska's most famous citizens. Pointing our rental car toward the airport, we were coming up on a busy Anchorage intersection when, without warning, a huge moose—A MOOSE!—came crashing out of the bushes.

She bolted across the four-lane road, inches away from becoming our hood ornament. We got a bird's-eye—make that moose's-eye—view of very long legs in motion, a hump behind her head just like in the pictures, and no antlers (she-moose don't have 'em). She sported more body than head and more legs than anything else.

Our only moose, in downtown Anchorage, of all places.

No one honked, no one braked, no one seemed surprised.

But those drivers were Alaskans. We were tourists. We were in hysterics. I was laughing so hard I had to lay my head on the steering wheel to catch my breath as our celebrity Alaskan cow disappeared into the nearby woods.

Maybe you're not heading quite that far north today, but that doesn't mean you won't see some very unusual sights outside your car window. Humor not only comes to those who wait but especially to those who look.

Lord, show me your ever-surprising world
through new eyes today.
Give me a glimpse of your holy sense of humor,
so apparent in your creation.
Moose, for example.
Let me wear my merry heart on my sleeve
and celebrate the banquet of joy spread before me,
a continual feast for my weary heart.

POSITIVELY THE PITS

In his kindness God called you to his eternal glory
by means of Jesus Christ.
After you have suffered a little while,
he will restore, support, and strengthen you,
and he will place you on a firm foundation.

—1 PETER 5:10 NLT

Some mornings are positively wonderful. And some are the pits.

Here's an honest word of encouragement for one of those pit-dwelling days.

Because the truth is, not a woman alive, including me, can sail through every minute of every day with a totally optimistic attitude, filled with love, joy, and peace. That's just not how real life works.

Here, for example, is a journal entry from one very bad day in August 1992 (yes, a full ten years after I gave my life to God), when my abundantly blessed body suddenly felt like a huge weight on my shoulders:

I am sick of being fat.
I am sick of thinking about it.

Tired of speaking about it. Don't want to write about it.
I am in pain and denial.
I don't know how to change.
I don't want to ask for help.

Look at all these negatives, Lord!
What happened to Lizzie?
Why won't this hurt go away?

I can't seem to find a "cause" for it.
A decision of the will to *make* it go away seems very temporary.

One day I think, "Terrific! I can embrace my fat self
and get on with life!" The next day (next hour?)
I am feeling awful about who I am, what I look like,
what I *feel* like.

I'm going for a walk. Don't go away, Lord.
I need you.

Oh, Lizzie.
I'm glad every day isn't like *that* day. But such low moments do come.

Being a Christian doesn't mean that our lives will be perfect, that problems are easily solved, or that we'll be filled with joy twenty-four hours a day. Everybody slips into a funk now and again. I'm simply on a mission to make sure we don't live there.

Our hope lies not in perfection but in perseverance and in our Lord Jesus who loves us "as is."

Lord, I remember that day and others like it.
And I remember days like this one,
when I'm so busy focused on ministering to others
that I forget to worry about myself.
This is better, Lord.
Forgive me when I throw a pity party,
especially when I drag in guests who don't want to be there.
Help me persevere, Lord,
despite my many imperfections

FALLING DOWN FUNNY

He will yet fill your mouth with laughing,
And your lips with rejoicing.

—*JOB 8:21*

Go ahead and yawn. Open wide, taking in some much-needed air. Now imagine your mouth filled with laughter. Delicious, isn't it? Few things are more fun than being so full of laughter that it spills out everywhere.

Kathleen overflowed quite by accident one day while sitting in an elegant hotel lobby in downtown Seattle, waiting for her husband to come out of a seminar. The magazine article she was reading included a photo of an X ray of a man's throat. It seemed he had swallowed a table knife while eating peas.

Suddenly, the very idea of such a ludicrous event washed over Kathleen, and she got seriously tickled. She bent over, laughing. She stood up, laughing. "It struck me so funny, I hugged the walls to keep upright while I found my way outside, passing a lobby filled with people staring at me as if to say, 'That woman has lost it!'"

Sitting outside on the front steps in her pretty spring dress, Kathleen laughed hysterically for the next twenty minutes.

Meanwhile, her husband heard about the crazy woman outside. When he realized it was his wife, he simply walked past her.

We've been there. Kathleen couldn't help herself. She literally had no control. Just like a child getting tickled physically, she got tickled mentally, with the same results. *Haaa!*

I've watched more than one woman in my audience get tickled. There she goes, bending over, red-faced, obviously having trouble breathing. Even as I continue telling some silly tale, I keep an anxious eye on her. *What's going on? Is she okay?*

Then my eyes widen. *Uh-oh.* The woman next to her is doing the same thing. It's contagious and headed in my direction. One by one, people fold over, lean back, fall sideways, turn colors, and gasp for breath.

Now and again some poor soul goes off the deep end and can't find her way back. Everyone around her begins to draw away, fearing the contagion. Try as she might, though, the afflicted woman can't pull herself together. Her loud whooping eases up for a breathless moment, then off she goes again.

Her friends shrug their shoulders. "She's not usually like this," they mouth carefully.

The rest of the audience stares at me. *Can't you do something about this?*

Do I have to? If I helped bring all this on, I love it.

In truth, it was her own fearfully and wonderfully made mind that went off on its own tangent. That's why she got tickled, never to return. I was merely a mirror, allowing her to discover something funny inside herself.

Today if the urge to fill your mouth with laughter strikes, open wide, sis.

Drink it in.

> *It feels so good to laugh, Lord,*
> *without worrying about how I look or what people think.*
> *They are probably wishing they were having*
> *half as much fun as we are.*

Do the Right(eous) Thing

If you abide in My word, you are My disciples indeed.
And you shall know the truth,
and the truth shall make you free.

—*John 8:31–32*

Four years of Latin come in handy once again: The word *disciple* means "one who learns by doing."

"Doing," eh? No wonder I struggle in my Christian walk. I'm trying to learn by *sitting!* Sitting in Sunday school, sitting in church, sitting at fellowship suppers. If you sit enough times in a row, you get a gold pin for perfect attendance. I've also tried to learn by *listening.* Listening to sermons and tape series and Christian radio and Christian speakers (yikes!). So much sound, most of it good, yet I'm still not made a disciple by listening.

Perhaps we learn by reading? Yes, yes, that's certainly the case as we read our Bibles and classic books of the faith. Surely reading is enough of a "doing" thing to lead to discipleship.

But . . . better is not best.

Gathering with the faithful, listening to solid teaching, and reading the Word of God are certainly good things. They just aren't the *only* things. They aren't even the *main* things. Jesus said, "*Abide in my word.*" That means live there, try it out, do what it says, get some obedience going in your life. Then you'll "know the truth" through experience rather than observation and be "free" of doubt and fear—a true disciple.

I used to say, "Wouldn't it have been easier to have lived when the disciples did, to have walked and talked with Jesus, to have experienced the Savior in person?"

In a word, no. First of all, with my "Question Authority" personality, I would have been a doubting Thomas, a denying Peter, or a persecuting Paul. As faithful disciples go, I'd have been one step above Judas. Maybe.

The twenty-first-century believer has several advantages over the first-century Christian. We have the gift of the Holy Spirit. We hold the printed Word of God in our hands. And we have two thousand years of changed lives as proof that Christianity is real and that being a disciple—learning by doing—is worth the effort.

Lord, help me do your Word,
not just read it.
Strengthen my resolve to,
above all things,
abide in you.

ZEAL APPEAL

Who is there to harm you
if you prove zealous for what is good?

—*1 Peter 3:13 NASB*

Zeal and enthusiasm are both well and good, but they have to be followed by positive action in the right direction. We are not called just to be zealous but to be zealous *for what is good*.

A few years into my radio career, I was called into my program director's office. I could see by his expression that he had something really exciting to share with me. "Liz, we've got a great idea for your midday show. Every Thursday, you'll be featuring an hour of call-ins with a psychic!"

The color drained out of my face. "A what?" I said weakly.

"A psychic." He extended her brochure in my direction. "I've heard she's really good."

"Do I have a choice about this?" I asked tentatively.

He was clearly taken aback. "Well . . . sure. It's your show. But psychics are really popular. Thousands of people will tune in to listen."

I took a deep breath. "Yes and millions of people read the *National Enquirer,* but that doesn't mean it's the truth." I had a desperate need to sit down before I fainted, but I stood my ground, literally and figuratively, even though I'd never opposed a boss like that.

We looked at one another, and then I knew. I'd won!

Better yet, Truth had won; Jesus had won.

"Okay," he said with a big sigh, "but I think you're missing a great opportunity to increase your ratings."

You know the rest of the story, don't you? The ratings went up all by themselves. With a little help from above. And that program director married a sister in Christ who got him straightened out, posthaste. Ain't life grand?

Sometimes you've got to be zealous for what is good and not worry about the outcome. When I go out on a limb, I ask myself, "What is the *worst* thing that could happen here?" Usually, it's not that bad. It's things like, "I'll be embarrassed"—well, that's nothing new. Or, "I'll lose their friendship"—risky, but many times by taking a stance you earn their respect and strengthen your friendship.

Then, I consider, "What is the *best* thing that could happen if I do this zealous, good thing?" Lives could be improved, hearts could be changed—it could be incredible!

Armed with such enthusiasm, we are to prove it, to put feet to our prayers and press on with perseverance. In response to our zeal, God makes a promise to us in the form of a question: "Who is there to harm you?" I knew I'd moved to a new place in my relationship with God when I realized I wasn't even afraid of death anymore. Oh, I'm still a little squeamish about how it will happen, and I wouldn't mind if he waited another forty years. But the fact is, I am not afraid of death because it's my ticket to *life*.

Lord, I want to be zealous for what is good,
trusting you with the outcome.
Help me be bold and fearless,
keeping my eyes on you.
Who can harm me when you are my shield?

A Kid's-Eye View

Blessed are the pure in heart,
For they shall see God.

—Matthew 5:8

Mothers wonder if their children comprehend spiritual truths. God, heaven, life, death—do they get this stuff? All those flannelboards on Sunday mornings, all those hours at Vacation Bible School—are the stories sinking in, taking root, making a difference?

I decided to find out and so asked Lillian, "Who rules the universe?"

"God does!" she answered promptly.

"Very good. But what about Jesus?"

She pondered briefly then announced, "They work together."

"Oh? What about the Holy Spirit?"

"He works on weekends!"

Truer words were never spoken.

On the day Lillian was baptized she was so excited she practically dived into the baptistry headfirst. I got wet too . . . with tears. Such a happy, happy day.

Drying her off after the big event, I reminded her gently, "Now the Lord lives in your heart."

Lillian nodded enthusiastically. "I can feel him rattling around in there already!" She suddenly pursed her lips together, squeezing out the words like toothpaste. "Do I have to keep my mouth closed so he won't get out?"

Now *there's* an idea.

A little girl named Carrie watched her mother get baptized and couldn't wait to tell the first person who asked her what happened: "The preacher threw Mommy in a big pot and washed all her skins away!" Then there was two-year-old Caitlin, on a road trip with her grandmother. Because of construction, they missed their exit. Her grandmother prayed out loud, "Lord, help us find our way."

Within a mile, they spotted a police officer and asked him for directions. Driving away, her grandmother prayed again, "Thank you, Lord, for taking care of us."

From the backseat, Caitlin's voice was filled with wonder. "Was that the Lord?"

Almost, sweet Caitlin.

Jesus said, "Whoever humbles himself as this little child is the greatest in the kingdom of heaven."[25] May we all listen carefully, watch closely, and take detailed notes as the children in our lives teach us to embrace life with innocence, humility, and childlike grace.

Lord Jesus, Caitlin was right:
You're everywhere,
looking out for my safety,
providing for me, loving me.
Give me the eyes of a child
to see you more clearly.

Just Let Go

Take My yoke upon you and learn from Me,
for I am gentle and lowly in heart,
and you will find rest for your souls.
For My yoke is easy and My burden is light.

—Matthew 11:29–30

Jesus wants us to slow down, find rest, release our burdens.

Yikes. We are moving far beyond my area of giftedness here.

My husband would agree: "No new projects!" he insists, as I wildly outline some urgent new idea or run off in yet another direction.

Such living catches up with me. Waking up in a hotel room in the dim hours of the morning, blind-as-a-bat Lizzie couldn't see the clock, but I could reach my watch. "Yee-oww!" I screamed, throwing myself over the edge of the bed and fumbling with the bedside lamp. "I'm late! I'm late!" I shrieked, sounding just like a certain rabbit from Wonderland.

Then, my myopic eyes focused on the alarm clock, and I realized it was an hour earlier than I'd feared, simply because I'd neglected to change my watch during my trip west. I wasn't late, I was on Central time. Sliding back into bed, I waited while my white rabbit heart slowed down enough for me to begin breathing again as I sought a few more minutes of "rest for my soul."

Prayer seems the logical path to these gentle words of Jesus beckoning us toward easier yokes and lighter burdens. The key, however, is in *sharing* our burdens with Christ and in yoking ourselves to him so that we walk *with* him rather than against him.

This sounds good in theory, yet it's tough for me to do in real life. Instead of praying, "Lord, thy will be done," it comes out more like, "Lord, *my* will be done, and the sooner the better!"

Flying off to a presentation, I pray (beg?) for the plane to land on schedule, when it might be more appropriate to pray for a calm spirit of resourcefulness, no matter what time it lands. On school mornings, when I run around the kitchen like a crazy woman trying to pack lunches and sign permission slips, I pray for help finding the children's library books, when a simple prayer for peaceful preparation the night before might have been a better move. Bill says I go through each day as if I'll never hit a red light. What he doesn't know is, I pray for green traffic lights too!

When I pray, "Lighten my load, Lord," the Lord's response is, *Take my yoke upon you and learn from me.* Wait a minute . . . take on more? No, take on a partner. By yoking myself with Jesus, my steps, by necessity, will become more "grace-full" as I learn how to follow his lead.

> Lord, when it comes to being yoked with you,
> I often behave like a dumb ox.
> I strain against your gentler pace and
> impatiently demand my own way.
> Teach me to let go of my need to control, Lord,
> and to trust you to guide me on the path to your glory.

Awe and Then Some

Charm is deceitful and beauty is passing,
But a woman who fears the Lord, she shall be praised.

—*Proverbs 31:30*

Don't let that "fear" thing frighten you, sis.

To "fear the Lord" means "to be in awe of, reverent toward." It's a healthy fear, considering his power. A recognition of his magnificence and might, which, once grasped, means less fear of everything else. Larry Eisenberg has the right idea: "For peace of mind, resign as general manager of the universe." Why not? The job has already been filled.

For me, to "fear the Lord" means to respect and love God so completely that I want to honor his goodness and grace with my life. I led a summer Bible study of Proverbs 31 and asked my attendees, "What is your greatest spiritual challenge?" Here's what they said:

"To keep growing in maturity instead of being too comfortable in my spiritual walk."

"To have a consistent quiet time."

"To be obedient to God's expressed will for my life."

"To concentrate on producing the fruit of the Spirit."

"To have a closer relationship with God in order to survive!"

Which of those resonates most with you this morning?

Singer and author Annie Chapman wrote that "the balanced woman is not out to please some of the people all of the time, or all of the people some of the time. Her strategy for living is to be simply, purely, passionately devoted to the Lord."[26]

Yes, yes, yes.

Tony Campolo is right: "When people recognize God as the ultimate Significant Other, they define their worth in terms of their relationship with Him."[27] And that relationship is meaningful to a vast number of people. A 1991 Roper poll asked a random sampling of men and women, "What is 'success'?" For both men and women, "being a good spouse and parent" was at the top of the list. Second on the list for women was "being true to God," more than twice as important to them as having knowledge, wealth, power, influence, or fame.

Our Proverbs 31 girlfriends from millennia past were right on target: Forget charm and beauty. God matters most.

I'm not scared of you, Lord.
Your perfect, unchanging, unconditional love
drives that fear right out of my heart.
But I stand in awe of you.
You are worthy to be first in all things, Jesus.
Whether I'm praised or not,
you should be.
Must be.

Wise with Years

Age should speak,
And multitude of years should teach wisdom.

—JOB 32:7

Growing older boils down to "good news" and "bad news."

Bad news? Skin tags. Facial hair. Varicose veins. You always wanted to grow up to be like your mom, right? You made it!

Good news? Wisdom. It only comes with age. You can't buy it, rent it, or surf your way to it on the Internet. Wisdom comes not from always doing things right but from living through doing them wrong and learning something in the process. I'm not all the way to wise yet, but I'm en route. So are you.

It's a trade-off: As our minds and hearts grow wiser, the rest of us grows rusty. Elbows, for example—a body part you hardly ever think about unless you bang it on a table (Ouch! Right on the funny bone!). It was precisely that not-so-funny bone that sent me to an orthopedist for the first time.

"Tennis elbow," he assured me, as he filled a hypodermic needle with cortisone.

I laughed. Loudly. "I haven't played tennis since I was eighteen!"

"Liz, that's what this injury is *called*, not what causes it," the doctor responded with a patient sigh. "You'll feel a little pressure now."

Another doctor had used those exact words when I was about to give birth to an almost twelve-pound baby, so I hung on to the examination table for dear life. When it turned out to be just that—a little pressure—I exhaled with relief and asked, "If this pain isn't caused by tennis, then what *has* happened?"

"You don't really want to hear it."

"It's *my* elbow. Of course I want to hear it."

Now that I've heard it, I never want to hear it again.

Trouble is, I *keep* hearing it from the lips of every professional person I visit: "Well, now that you're over forty . . ."

My optometrist said it when she intoned that dreaded word *bifocals.*

My dentist said it when she gently pointed out my "receding gum line."

My internist said it when she discussed the concept of "zero metabolism."

My gynecologist said it when she whispered ominously, "premenopausal."

My hairstylist said it when she tried to fluff hair that's no longer there due to "hormonal hair loss."

My cosmetician said it while she plucked and clucked over "hormonal hair *gain.*"

Welcome to life on the other side of the big 4-0.

As a junior student of the Scriptures, I'm curious about one thing:

Why is forty such a hot item in the Bible? For the definitive answer, I turned to my hubby, Bill, who has a Ph.D. in Old Testament Languages (long story). He explained that forty is a very significant number—an entire generation. It's also the age at which a person was considered "full grown." (Good, because this is as full as I want to get.)

Forty was how long critical situations lasted—testings, trials (that flood thing, for Noah), and temptations. In those days, if you made it through to forty-one, the light from the Promised Land was on the horizon. (Unless you were Moses, in which case the light was a burning bush.)

For the rest of us, that light is the blaze from the candles on our birthday cakes, setting off smoke alarms. Grab a fire extinguisher and press on, sis!

Lord Jesus, it's hard to watch these bodies,
which we've come to know and trust,
become unfamiliar and undependable.
All the more reason to
depend on you.
Someday when we pass from forty to glory,
seeing your timeless face
will be all that matters.

Sizing Things Up

I will praise You, for I am fearfully and wonderfully made;
Marvelous are Your works,
And that my soul knows very well.

—Psalm 139:14

People magazine once featured a cover story entitled "Diet Wars: Who's Winning, Who's Sinning." Featured on the cover? Oprah Winfrey, Liz Taylor, and Delta Burke. "Sinners," I suppose. The article also featured Roseanne Arnold and Dolly Parton, among others, and closed with these words: "In our society, is there such a thing as fat and happy?"

Excuse me while I shout: "Yes! Wonderfully happy!"

But what about that "sinning" part? Those of us who are concerned about righteousness (as opposed to *self*-righteousness) often take to heart the suggestion that being bigger than average is somehow a sin. One woman wrote me:

> *Try to convince me I'm not a fat, ugly slob. I struggle spiritually with this . . . gluttony is listed in the Word as a sin . . . I can't seem to "mortify" this as instructed in Romans 8:13.*

Oh, dear sister. You are not a "fat, ugly slob." You might simply be a large woman. Is that so awful? Words like *big* and *large* can mean very positive things: powerful, mighty, generous, magnificent, spacious, vast, towering, impressive, boundless, substantial, stately, and great!

As to her spiritual struggle, though I found lots of references in the Bible to "appetite," they pointed not merely to food but to all the fleshly desires. Such appetites can be found in thin people too.

What the Bible does speak against is overeating (and overdrinking) to the point of inebriation. In Proverbs, it says:

> *Do not mix with winebibbers,*
> *Or with gluttonous eaters of meat;*
> *For the drunkard and the glutton will come to poverty,*
> *And drowsiness will clothe a man with rags.*[28]

Sinful to overeat? Yes, if you're so "drunk" with food that it's hard to function. Like after Thanksgiving dinner, when we really have eaten too much and stretch our swollen stomachs across the couch, moaning about that last slice of pumpkin pie. Both the Great Physician and your family doctor would agree: "All things in moderation."

Sinful to be fat, though? I don't think so. Being large doesn't necessarily mean you are a glutton. Some of us overeat, some don't. An athlete who eats 5,000 calories a day isn't considered a glutton, because his or her body will burn every one of those calories. Perhaps it's not our eating that's to blame one iota for our size. Could be a little more physical exertion is called for. Could be genes. Could be metabolism. Could be a dozen reasons, most of them beyond our jurisdiction.

It comes down to this, beloved: If you are eating too much, too often . . . well, you know what to do.

But if you are simply larger than the other women in your pew, even though you eat intelligently . . . well, you also know what to do. See yourself as fearfully and wonderfully made by the Lord, who loves all women, of all sizes, without discrimination.

> It sounds too good to be true, Lord.
> Yet you are the definition of all that is good
> and just and loving.
> Show me where I am off the mark, Father,
> those things that need changing, adjusting, discarding.
> Give me the strength to take whatever steps are necessary.
> Then help me accept the finished product
> as your gift to me. As something good.
> No . . . as something wonderful, Lord.
> Just like you.

PRAYER CHANGES THINGS

Or what man is there among you who, if his son asks for bread,
will give him a stone? Or if he asks for a fish, will he give him a serpent?
If you then, being evil, know how to give good gifts to your children,
how much more will your Father who is in heaven
give good things to those who ask Him!

—MATTHEW 7:9–11

See if this prayer-time scenario rings a familiar bell, my sister.

It was a sunny Saturday morning, and I was headed for our neighborhood antique store, praying that the deacon's bench I'd seen on display a week before was still for sale. *It would look so nice on our screened porch, Lord,* I prayed as I stepped inside the dimly lit shop. *Please let the bench still be there.*

My heart did a flip: There it sat, waiting for me. *What a blessing!* I thought, smiling warmly as I got out my checkbook while the owner loaded the bench into my van. *It was meant to be,* I reasoned. *After all, it's a deacon's bench—there must be something spiritual about that!*

Nice try, Liz.

Then there are those prayers that amount to little more than calling out for help at every inconvenience as I barrel along on my own agenda. Like a child stamping her foot, my prayers end up sounding like, "I want it fixed, I want it right, I want it now!" And while adding "please" may be polite and ending my request with "in Jesus' name" may sound pious—neither phrase helps if the thing I'm praying for is less than divine.

Childlike prayers are fine.

Childish prayers are a whine.

By the time she was five, my daughter had already earned a black belt in shopping, thanks to a mother who found it hard to say no to her plaintive pleas for this or that little toy. "Oh, Mama!" she'd say dramatically. "I really need this!"

"No," I'd say, "you mean you really want it. There's a difference." At which I'd be brought up short, realizing how similar my prayers must sound sometimes.

Determining what qualifies as a need rather than a want is tricky territory. Yes, I need a roof over my head, but just how nice a roof is it appropriate to pray for? Sure, I need clothing to cover my body, but does praying for a gorgeous sweater to appear on the sale rack make spiritual sense?

Ask five Christians and you'll hear five different opinions on this one. For me, I keep coming back to Jesus' challenge: "But seek first the kingdom of God and His righteousness, and all these things shall be added to you."[29] When I make my time alone with God and his Word a daily priority, I find my choices about wants vs. needs amazingly easy. When I get lazy or careless about that quiet time, I find myself struggling with every purchase, every decision.

We know the Lord loves to hear the prayers of his children and wants us to "pray without ceasing." But prayer without seeking, knocking, and finding his will for us ultimately frustrates us and leaves us wondering, *Doesn't God care?* He cares very much—but more for our hearts than our wish lists.

God isn't Santa; he's Savior. What he saves us from isn't only death but from ourselves and from our foolish, selfish desires. Lately I've discovered a new meaning for the small sign that's been hanging in my office for years. It says simply, "Prayer Changes Things."

Indeed. What prayer changes is me.

Lord, thank you for listening to my prayers
even when I sound like a spoiled, selfish child.
Teach me the difference between my wants
and my needs,
between the desires of my flesh
and the desires of your heart.
You do give us wonderful gifts, Father God,
not one more precious than your Son.

DRESSED FOR SUCCESS

Strength and honor are her clothing.

—PROVERBS 31:25A

Anything in your closet this morning that fits the above definition for a well-dressed woman?

My friend Cheryl discovered her attire was neither strong nor honorable when she made the mistake of getting dressed while her five-year-old daughter watched intently.

"Mommy," the child asked, "why is the skin on your tummy all wrinkly like that?"

Cheryl explained, "My tummy had to stretch a lot when I was carrying you and your brothers before you were born, so the skin never quite went all the way back."

Her daughter pondered that explanation for a moment. "Kinda like a balloon that's lost its air, huh?"

"Uh . . . yes, dear, kind of like that."

"But, Mommy." She pointed to Cheryl's legs. "Why are your knees all wrinkly?"

Cheryl looked down at her saggy knees. "Well, honey, that's what happens to your skin when you get a little older."

"Will your whole body get like that?" Her daughter eyed her up and down. "I guess your skin just gets tired and gives up, huh?"

Yes, child, that's pretty much how it works.

Ah, but it's how we *clothe* our skin that matters most.

Take that woman in Proverbs 31, for example. She knew how to dress for success, donning strength like a shield. In the Hebrew, the word *strength* means "mighty fortress, powerful stronghold." It's not *our* meager strength that's needed here . . . it's God's. Think of Martin Luther's old German hymn, "A Mighty Fortress Is Our God." Dressed in God's strength, I am ready to face whatever the day holds, including curious kids and stubborn wrinkles.

The ideal woman of Proverbs 31 was also clothed in *honor*—in Hebrew, "dignity, splendor, majesty, and beauty." Words that suit our glorious Lord much more than they'd ever describe most of us, even in our finest garb.

What makes this godly attire especially attractive is the combination: strength *and* honor. We've all known women who were strong but not very honorable. Our television screens are filled with them. And there are women who are honorable but, frankly, not very strong. The first setback or the first perceived threat, and they fold up like a card table.

The kind of women most of us long to be are both strong and honorable, clothed with the kind of power that comes from on high, certain of our value in God's eyes, definite in our calling, and moving forward with complete assurance.

Francis de Sales said it best: "Nothing is so strong as gentleness, nothing so gentle as real strength."

As I gaze into my closet this morning, Lord,
looking for something to wear,
remind me of the heavenly wardrobe available to me.
Forgive me when I clothe myself in my own strength
or seek after my own honor,
when you alone can wrap me in both,
from head to toe.

THE PRESSURE IS OFF

For the sake of my brethren and companions,
I will now say, "Peace be within you."

—PSALM 122:8

My friend Candy from Maryland says, "If you're burning the candle at both ends, you're not as bright as you think!" The good news is, as each year goes by, you can blow out more than the candles on your cake; you can blow out that candle burning at the other end of your busy day. You can get up early or you can stay up late, but you don't need to do both because, honey, peace is yours and the pressure is *off*.

Everyone tells you about wrinkles and hot flashes (including me), but here's the *real* surprise that arrives once you reach forty: The pressure to be perfect (most of which was self-imposed anyway) has diminished, and you can finally be *you!*

Hollywood celebrities, especially female ones, never have the freedom that you and I have just to "be." The fame and fortune of, say, Cindy Crawford, have so revolved around her looks that until the day they take her away in a pine box, people will be commenting on her appearance. Elizabeth Taylor's figures have been more closely watched than the stock market. Oprah's ratings have gone up and down and so has her scale, all observed by the unforgiving eye of the viewing public.

Lucky us! Nobody is watching. I mean *nobody*. The pressure began lifting at age thirty, moving off so slowly, so quietly, that we almost didn't notice. Suddenly, at forty we became aware of this new freedom and a whole new set of (lower) expectations.

I got a firsthand glimpse of the over-forty attitude in action years ago when my sister Sarah and I went to a very nice restaurant in Louisville. The line to the ladies' room was long and slow (what's new?), but the men's room seemed deserted.

"Cover me!" Sarah said and ducked into the doorway marked Men.

"Cover her?" What is this, a James Bond movie? I was beyond embarrassed and ran to our table to wait for her, hoping no one noticed that we were even together. Today, I would be the first one to whip open the door and announce, "We're coming in!"

Here's the most quietly exciting reason why life after forty is so peace-filled: When we let go of judging others, we also let go of judging ourselves. Losses and changes have taught us the value of appreciation and gratitude. So what if we don't look as good as we did at twenty? We are thinking and acting *much better!*

As the wise preacher once said, "That which is has already been, /And what is to be has already been."[30]

Or, as Doris Day put it, "Que Sera, Sera!"

What a relief, Lord Jesus!
To shake off some of that pressure to look and be perfect,
and simply look—and be—me.
What peace it is not to judge,
nor be judged.
To appreciate what I have,
rather than mourn what I no longer have.
Thank you for letting me live long enough
to learn this lesson:
R-E-L-A-X.

Be Still, Beloved

The LORD your God in your midst,
The Mighty One, will save;
He will rejoice over you with gladness,
He will quiet you with His love,
He will rejoice over you with singing.

—*ZEPHANIAH 3:17*

Imagine this: The Lord, the Mighty One, in your midst right now—seated across from you at the kitchen table or perched on the arm of your favorite overstuffed chair—quieting you with his love, whispering sweet somethings in your ear, singing gentle songs of peace, joy, and gladness.

Imagine how it would make you feel: So safe. So secure. So calm. So relaxed.

So the opposite of how we usually live.

Dashing around my home office one overcommitted day, I didn't notice the sheet of clear plastic bubble wrap that waited innocently in my path. When my size-ten feet hit those tiny, tightly sealed air bubbles, sharp popping sounds like ricocheting bullets rang through the tile-floored office.

"W-a-a-a!!" I shrieked, instinctively jumping from one foot to the other, trying to make the mysterious floor-level explosions go away. I stopped jumping and dared to look down, muttering, "What in the world . . . "

At that moment, Bill came tearing into the room, having heard the terrible noise and expecting the worst. "What happened?" he shouted. Then he looked at my feet.

The room was filled with more noise than ever—but this time, it was the sound of laughter. As I picked up what was left of the bubble packing, I said with a sheepish grin, "I think the Lord just burst my, 'Out of my way, I'm in a hurry' bubble!"

You can never learn this lesson too early in life.

When my Lillian was eight, I overheard her calling up a friend, only to learn from the girl's mother that she was out for the afternoon.

"Oh my," Lillian sighed. "When will she be back?"

Clearly it was going to be many hours later, and the mother must have asked Lillian if she wanted to leave a message. This was a new concept for my daughter.

"A message?" Lillian said, dumbfounded. "Well . . . tell her to put my foot in her prayers."

A big *"haaawww!"* slipped out of my mouth before I could stop it. (I've heard of putting your foot in your mouth, but in your *prayers*?)

"Mo-ther!" Lillian whined, stamping her foot. The same foot she'd supposedly hurt a week earlier, the one with the Ace bandage, the one that she'd danced on seconds ago without so much as a wince. Her prayer-request foot.

She returned to her phone conversation with a sniff. "Tell Morgan to put my foot in her prayers, and I'll call back later." At which point she might throw in the other foot to keep things hopping.

For my Lillian and for me—and perhaps for you, dear sister—it's time to slow down, to cease hopping impatiently from one foot to the other. Because while we're busily dancing, the Lord is quietly singing. I don't want to miss the music . . . do you?

Oh, Lord! To think of you
caring enough to quiet me with your love.
What a heavenly caress, what sweet words!
Help me sit still in your presence.
Help me relax completely.
Help me simply wait
and listen.

Take a Deep Breath

And His name will be called
Wonderful, Counselor, Mighty God,
Everlasting Father, Prince of Peace.

—Isaiah 9:6b

Come January, some women choose a verse for the year, or a famous quote, or a line of poetry. I keep it simple. I choose one word.

Peace was the word I chose several years ago. During those twelve months, I found I could experience peace anytime, anywhere, by doing two things: praying and breathing in unison.

Choose a straight-back chair, set your feet on the floor, and place your hands in your lap or by your side. Silence helps but isn't necessary, because I've done this in crowded airports or at the dinner table when the conversation sounded more like war than peace.

Breathe deeply and evenly, through your nose, all the way down to the base of your spine. When you can hold no more, pause for a beat or two and begin to let the air out v-e-r-y slowly through your mouth. Just open your lips and let it flow out; no need to hiss and blow like the wind, just nice and easy. I love to meditate on this verse while I'm at it: "Peace I leave with you, My peace I give to you,"[31] or another favorite, "And let the peace of God rule in your hearts."[32]

After a mad dash for a tight connection on Delta, I dropped into seat 14-C and knew I needed God's peace ASAP. I closed my eyes and began to breathe slowly and intentionally. Soon I had the distinct sensation of moving forward. *We're headed for the runway already,* I thought and opened my eyes. We hadn't moved an inch! The plane was sitting absolutely still, but I was moving all right . . . toward peace.

Just as we are sometimes encouraged to tighten all our muscles, then relax them one by one as a method of physical stress reduction, I have found the same concept works with thoughts of peacefulness.

First, think of all the words that are the *opposite* of peace: *shouting, turmoil, chaos, conflict, hostility, violence, pain, suffering, war, death.* Ugh.

Then, concentrate on peaceful words: *quiet, calm, contentment, serenity, tranquillity, harmony, healing, relief, life, love, Jesus.* Ahhh.

He is the Prince, the Ruler, the Sovereign of Peace. Real peace can only come from him. Anything else, even breathing, is temporary and of the flesh. It's just an aid to get you where you want to be: in his peaceful presence.

Lord, thank you for bringing peace
right to the doorstep of my heart.
Help me breathe it in, hold it close,
and release it peacefully to all who surround me.
I'm grateful peace is contagious, Lord.
This year and always,
let there be peace on earth.

Welcome to Simplicity

. . . you will receive a rich welcome
into the eternal kingdom
of our Lord and Savior Jesus Christ.

—*2 Peter 1:11 NIV*

Come with me to Shaker Village of Pleasant Hill, Kentucky. These devout believers were known for the saying, "We make you kindly welcome." And how do they make you welcome? Quietly. The last living Kentucky Shaker left this earth in 1923.

Yet welcome they still do. Their all-white walls say, "Welcome to a place that is clean." Scrubbed daily and painted white again when a scrub brush can't get them clean anymore they are a gentle reminder that our sins, red as scarlet, are made white as snow.

The straight edges of Shaker furniture say, "Welcome to a place where beauty is found in a straight line." No distracting curves or garish ornamentation to mislead the mind. Here, the surfaces are smooth, the horizontal and the vertical. The One who makes the crooked places straight would feel most welcome in this land of lines.

The horizontal band of pegs that rings the rooms says, "Welcome to a place of order." Chairs, hangers, and candleholders are all designed to hang from large wooden pegs. A place for everything, where all questions have answers. "Where do I hang my hat?" Kindly hang it here.

The sparse furnishings say, "Welcome to a place where you can breathe." Every graphic artist will recognize it as three-dimensional white space. There is room for the senses to regroup, free of assault. Simple white curtains open to pastoral views, a feast for tired eyes.

The Shaker silence, broken only by a softly closed door or faint step in the hall, says, "Welcome to a place of solitude." Thick walls and surrounding fields keep the din of a noisy, modern world at bay. Here is a refuge of quiet and peacefulness. The soul revels in the stillness.

A distant dinner bell says, "Welcome to a place of repast." The meals are full of simple goodness. No gourmet sauces, no continental seasonings. Just what the body needs and nothing more, delicious in its simplicity.

The tall bed, so high it requires a footstool to climb aboard, says, "Welcome to a place of rest." Beneath the plain white coverlet and clean white sheets, the restoration of sleep awaits. Those who are heavy laden will find rest.

Every corner of Shaker Village is a prayer closet, created with as few distractions as possible. At any moment you can drop to your knees and find God waiting in the silence and saying, "We make you kindly welcome."

Lord, teach me what the Shakers knew
about simplicity.
Help me clear away
the distractions of life
and find you in the sacred stillness,
in the straight lines of a clean and orderly life,
in the breathing space of solitude and rest.
Lord, welcome me into your waiting arms.

Get Over It

Most of the time I live like an overwhelmer rather than an over-comer. With a too busy schedule and too few hours, I run around like the proverbial headless chicken, about to collapse. It's a sure thing that when my stress builds up, I get in big trouble.

One afternoon, with a plane to catch and much left to pack, I tore into the house through the kitchen and promptly knocked over the cat's milk dish. I don't mean I bumped it, I mean I *launched* it with my toe. Milk went all over my freshly mopped floor, even as our cleaning pro was pulling out of the driveway.

Furthermore, I now had warm milk all over my nice new shoes. Not water, which might dry unnoticed. Milk.

Needless to say, I was not happy, blessed, or feeling like an overcomer. This was not the first time I'd knocked over the cat dish, just the worst time. Thinking the house was empty, I shouted at the top of my lungs, "That #$%&! will have to go somewhere else!"

At that exact moment, the door to our downstairs bathroom

began to swing open, and the face of our house painter appeared, wide-eyed and fear-stricken.

My own face was now beet red. I stammered, "Oh! No, no, not you! You are welcome to go . . . anywhere you like. I was talking to the cat dish."

The what?

"Sure, ma'am." He slid past me, then bolted for the back door and certain safety.

I slumped into a chair, embarrassed—laughing at my foolishness, yet deeply ashamed by my lack of control. *Why can't I overcome, Lord? Why do I succumb to old habits? Why don't I "let go and let God," instead of letting 'er rip?*

Oh, wretched woman that I certainly am. Who will get me out of this mess? The ultimate Overcomer. My Lord and Savior, who forgives me when I fail yet persuades me to press on for higher ground.

Lord, what would I do without you
to pick me up and push me forward,
up and over the cares of this world?
As always, I throw myself at your mercy,
deserving not a drop of it
but grateful beyond measure.

P.S. In case you were worried, I tracked down the painter and asked his forgiveness too!

Have a Midlife Cry, Sis

Do not cast me off in the time of old age;
Do not forsake me when my strength fails.

—PSALM 71:9

It's been said that midlife is when your broad mind and your narrow waist change places. I'm not sure where that leaves me, since my waist hasn't been narrow since 1968 and my broad mind is what got me in trouble before I let the Lord take the wheel.

Forty is far from being old. At least that's what I keep telling myself. It's also far from being young. Young is two hours of sleep and no makeup. Old is also two hours of sleep and no makeup. Forty is smack in the middle: eight hours of sleep, a midday nap, and tons of makeup.

Donna loves this middle ground of life: "No matter what you say or do, it can be explained away, 'I'm in midlife crisis!'"

I'm not in a crisis; I'm in denial. On those mornings when I creak out of bed and shuffle down the hall, I keep telling myself, "Relax, Liz. Any day now, you'll feel as good as ever. This has just been a stressful week."

Right.

The forties are an awkward time of social adjustment, trying to figure out where one "fits" in the grand scheme of things. In our teens, we're busy making friends. In our twenties, we're making our move up the ladder of career success. In our thirties, we're making money and, perhaps, a name for ourselves. Then, in our forties, we're trying to make sense of it all, especially if we haven't amassed the fame, fortune, or friends we'd hoped for.

At forty, life not only pulls the rug out from under us, it knocks out two walls and puts in a skylight. The world doesn't look right anymore. We say things like, "Is it my imagination, or is the HR department hiring them younger every year?"

The people we've always looked up to—physicians, airline pilots, professors, those older role models, those paragons of maturity—suddenly look too young to be in charge. Even worse, these young whippersnappers (I've always wanted to use that word) seem to be doing *better* than we are. Driving through a high-ticket subdivision, I mutter to myself, "How can couples in their thirties afford a house like that?"

Easy: At twenty-five, I went to parties. They went to med school.

I find myself sitting on planes next to women with nicer clothes, fancier laptop computers, and better jewelry, and then realize they are fifteen years younger than I am.

Oh help, Lord! Is this how it's going to be?

Yes and no. Yes, our coworkers and caretakers are getting younger every year. No, we don't have to get depressed about it. Soon enough, it will be their turn to have a midlife crisis. Then we can pass them a tissue, pat their hand, and say, "Have a good cry, sis."

Lord, there is no crisis
too big for you to handle.
Help me find the fun in all things,
but especially in growing older.
Our culture worships young faces and lean bodies, Lord.
But your Word honors wisdom and maturity.
Help me to give in to neither foolish denial nor hopeless despair
but to find that happy middle ground of acceptance.

Harvest Time

Therefore, if anyone is in Christ, he is a new creation;
old things have passed away; behold, all things have become new.

—*2 Corinthians 5:17*

On the February weekend in 1982 when I received Christ, you can imagine what my coworkers thought when this party-hearty woman danced out the door Friday afternoon heading for a bar and danced in Monday morning saying, "Praise the Lord, I've been baptized!"

People notice stuff like that.

They watched me like a hawk as spring turned into summer while I soared and stumbled along my new walk with Christ. A curious cohort, who'd observed my metamorphosis from wild woman to enthusiastic believer, asked me one autumn day, "Liz, what does it mean to be a Christian?"

Glancing at a ceramic pumpkin perched on her desk, I said brightly, "Oh, it's just like being a pumpkin!"

"Really?" she asked. "What do you mean by that?"

I gulped, having no earthly idea what I meant. There I was, trying to answer the most important question a person can ever ask, and I was in trouble with a capital *T* and that rhymes with *P* and that stands for pumpkin!

Lord, please help this make sense.

I took a deep breath and a broad leap of faith. "First, God brings us into his house out of the pumpkin patch of life."

"No kidding?" My friend nodded thoughtfully. "Tell me more."

"More?" *Gulp.* "Now we have a choice—bake in an oven, or be turned into something brand-new."

"I vote for brand-new," she said.

So far, so good. "Because we're filthy from rolling around in the dirt, God washes us on the outside. That's like baptism. Then he pierces our thick skins with the double-edged sword of his Word so he can clean out all that yucky stuff."

She made a face. "Pumpkins are so slimy on the inside."

"Slimy as sin," I agreed. "And full of seeds of bitterness and discontent that cling to our lives. Thank goodness God is willing to do it, because he's the only One who can make us clean, inside and out."

"Then what?"

"He gives us a brand-new face! Eyes that see like his, without blinking or turning away. A nose to capture the fragrant aroma of his sacrifice. And a mouth that smiles with joy."

My friend was the one smiling now.

"Finally, he puts the light of his Spirit in us and puts us out in a dark world to shine for him."

Her eyes widened. "Boy, that makes so much sense!"

I'll say. My hands were shaking as I reached for a pencil. *Maybe I'd better write this down . . .*

More than a dozen years later, my published version came rolling off the press—*The Pumpkin Patch Parable*—a "how to be made into a new creation" book for kids. Since the Lord himself created pumpkins, it made sense to redeem this familiar symbol of the harvest season for his good purpose.

Celebrate Halloween? No way. Celebrate a life surrendered to Christ? Any day of the year.

True confession, Lord:
It was frightening
to let you inside my dark heart.
I was sure my past would scare you away
forever.
But you plunged your holy hands into that unholy mess
and made my heart clean.
Please do it again, Lord.
Create a clean heart in me this day
so I may shine brighter for your glory.

BACK TO BASICS

Therefore know that the LORD your God, He is God,
the faithful God who keeps covenant and mercy
for a thousand generations with those who love Him
and keep His commandments.

—DEUTERONOMY 7:9

God is such a good name for God. It's only one syllable but a powerful one, full of strong, guttural sounds that come from the chest when you say it: "God."

It appears some four thousand times in Scripture and is the name you probably use most when speaking about him. After all, it's a safe name, a starting point with people. I'll often say, "God bless you," to someone as a word of encouragement and see how it's received. *God* is universal enough to not rattle too many cages.

It's usually the name we teach a child to say first. Concepts of God's Son and Spirit will come later, but first, God. When Matthew was just learning to read, he had a wipe-clean book (the only kind a three-year-old should have!) called *Thank You, God*. That was the sum of its message. A picture of an orange; "Thank you, God, for oranges." A picture of a cat; "Thank you, God, for cats." And so on. Matthew really got into it and would look out the car window and shout, "Thank you, God, for trees! Thank you, God, for stop signs! Thank you, God, for garbage trucks!"

I tried not to laugh as I started to correct him. "Matthew, we don't have to thank God for everything." Then I stopped myself. Why not? If we're to give thanks in all things, who says garbage trucks don't count?

Thank you, God . . . for everything.

Our God is definitely God with a big G, not any mere god of our own understanding. We're surrounded by people who worship a god of their personal creation, a god who answers to their own description. The difference between G and g is subtle, yet critical.

Soon after giving my life to Christ, I was speaking to a group of high school students, encouraging them to seek God's strength through the tough years ahead. A local politician came up to shake my hand afterward. "I'm with you," he said. "Kids need something to hang their hats on, and I don't care what god it is."

"But which God they choose is everything," I said slowly, watching his eyes. "Do you hope for righteous, loving kids?" When he nodded enthusiastically, I added, "Then they need to worship a righteous, loving God—not a Santa Claus god or a Feel Good god, but God as he reveals himself in his Word."

I'm not certain he was convinced. But I am.

Lord, if a child can say,
"Thank you, God!" for everything,
let me always do the same.
Help me boldly speak your name in every situation,
knowing that you are the one true God.

FADE TO BLACK

Now the eyes of Israel were dim with age, so that he could not see.

GENESIS 48:10A

See? See what? The big *E* on the chart?

Uh-oh.

The brochure at my optometrist's office made it all sound so simple: "If you're over 40 and are having trouble reading up close, you probably have a common and natural condition called *presby-opia*." (Sounds more like the fear of becoming a Presbyterian.)

On the day that bifocals showed up at my life's doorstep, my eye doctor, a pretty thirty-something redhead with flawless skin and perfect vision, leaned over, patted my hand, and said softly, "It's time, Liz."

I could feel the tears rising in my throat. Blinking and swallowing, I plastered my face with a big, brave smile. "Great!" I said, but didn't mean it.

"You'll learn to love bifocals," she said and didn't mean that either.

I ordered the "Progressive Addition Lenses" (the kind without the line), which the brochure insisted would give me "a full range of uninterrupted vision, more like the natural vision of your youth."

Can't they do better than that? By the time I was twenty, my eyes tested at 20/350. I want the natural vision of a young woman who can see herself in the mirror from across the sink, something I've never experienced as an adult.

After tripping my way up and down the steps for a few weeks, I went back to my optometrist and asked if contact lenses were out of the question. She smiled brightly and said, "Oh no, we'd be happy to fit you with some new lenses that match your bifocal prescription. We call these monovision lenses." Drop the first two letters and it's close to the mark: NOvision.

One contact uses your close-up prescription, good for reading or threading a needle. The other contact is for long-distance viewing, like driving a car or identifying that woman across the room who's talking to your husband. A great concept, in theory. The problem is they expect you to wear both contact lenses *at the same time!*

I asked my doctor, "How will this work?"

She said, "Relax. Your brain will adjust."

Adjust to what? With bifocals I move my head up and down, up and down. With monovision contacts, I shift my head back and forth, back and forth. Much too confusing for my addled brain.

Still, if you can see well enough to read this page—even with trifocals tipped back and an arm extender—thank the Lord you can see at all. One Alabama woman had an experience that has taught her much about what it means to be able to clearly see what matters most:

"Last summer I lost the vision in my right eye, with a 30 percent possibility of also losing my left eye vision. I really wasn't discouraged.

I just considered it too big for me to handle. A friend commented, 'I don't understand how God could have allowed this to happen to you.' Searching for the words to help her understand, I said, 'Think of it this way . . . I just see a little less of a man so I can see a little more of God.'"

That's what I call 20/20 vision, beloved.

Give me eyes to see
the things that matter, Lord.
Important things like
a wounded heart that needs mending.
A lonely soul who needs cheering up.
A neglected child who needs hugging.
As long as I have sight,
let me read your Word
and write it on the tablet of my heart
for that someday when the pages blur for good.
Open my eyes, Lord.
I want to see Jesus.

Did You Feel That?

And so it is written,
The first man Adam was made a living soul;
the last Adam was made a quickening spirit.

—1 Corinthians 15:45 KJV

"Quickening" is the medical term for the first moment when a woman feels her not-yet-born baby move inside her. The first sensation of life, of activity, of certain growth.

Sure, we can hear the heartbeat weeks earlier. *Whoosh-up. Whoosh-up.* Scared me silly. I prayed like mad that I wouldn't give birth to a whale.

Then we can see an ultrasound image, that pie-shaped picture on the screen, that womb with a view. "There are the feet," the technician says, pointing authoritatively while I'm counting six feet and at least two heads.

Is it human? we wonder. *Is it alive?*

That's why the quickening is so vital. Alive and kicking, yes indeed.

With my first child, that official quickening happened at a convention in Atlanta. At the end of a whirlwind day of meeting dozens of speakers and hearing the best of the best, I was stretched out on my bed, too excited to sleep, when suddenly it happened. *Ba-thwump. Ba-thwumpity-thwump.*

What was that? I thought, fearing the worst. When it happened a third time—that subtle but distinct sensation of movement, like waves through water—I knew.

Now, my *heart* went *ba-thwump*. Life—inside me! If I close my eyes right now, I can still feel that first quickening and the once-in-a-lifetime thrill that came with it.

What other ways might we connect with this idea of quickening?

When I answer the phone and hear my sweet Bill's voice on the other end of the line, my heart quickens. It literally picks up the pace, and I feel a lightness in my chest. "After all those years of marriage?" you ask. Yes indeed.

And when I'm in a crowd and hear someone speak the name of Jesus, I instinctively turn in that direction and feel the same warm stirring in the center of my being. *She's talking about the One I love!* And when I have a sense of his presence in worship, or when I am interceding for someone in prayer and sense his words of encouragement coming from my lips, it generates that quickening—that "life-giving spirit"[33]—inside my soul.

Ooh baby.

There really is a difference between the quick and the dead.

Lord, keep me ever alert to even the slightest move
of your Holy Spirit in me
so that I might respond
quickly.
Help me listen for the sound of your voice
in the stillness of my soul,
and look for the signs of your life-giving Spirit
in the eyes of those around me.
Let me always celebrate the joy of being
born again.

By the Dawn's Early Light

I am the Root and the Offspring of David,
the Bright and Morning Star.

—*Revelation 22:16b*

The morning star is the one that shines in the eastern sky just before dawn. Some say it's Venus, lit by the sun. For this girl, though, "morning star" means something even more glorious, a glistening memory from my childhood.

Growing up in Lititz, a quaint town in the heart of the Pennsylvania German farmlands, I was destined to be a Lutheran or a Moravian. My father chose the Moravian congregation, no doubt because it was the oldest in town. And oh, what a sanctuary!

It is, first and foremost, a place of beauty. An old-fashioned, churchy-looking church, planted among the majestic trees and verdant grass along Main Street. Tall, narrow stained-glass windows point to the steeple, which points to God.

Inside, winding staircases lead to the balcony where a huge, historic organ holds court. The Moravians love their music—great

German hymns and stirring compositions with lots of brass instruments and big choirs.

One Moravian song in particular stands out because it was sung by the children's choir on Christmas Eve: "Morning Star, O Cheering Sight!"

Unbeknownst to me in my youth, to be chosen as soloist for "Morning Star" was a big deal. Since I didn't know that, I auditioned fearlessly and was chosen to sing it the year I turned seven. Of course, my parents insisted I was the best "Morning Star" soloist ever. (Don't let their opinion sway yours!)

As I've watched my own children grow up, I'm amazed I ever had the nerve to stand up in our tall white church at that young age and make a sound! It's obvious why they wanted a child for the part, though: The gentle music and sweet words are made more so when heard in the high, thin, tender voice of a youngster.

We are not Moravians now, so Lillian will never be the "Morning Star" girl. But she *was* the recipient of the "Sunbeam for Jesus" award. Her last day of kindergarten, she was presented with an official-looking certificate declaring her to be a "Sunbeam." I gave her a big hug when she returned to her seat, a bright yellow poster in hand.

On the drive home from school that day, I asked her, "What does it mean to be a 'Sunbeam for Jesus'?"

Lillian was quiet for a moment, then confessed, "I guess it means I'm shiny."

"Is Jesus shiny too?" I asked.

She nodded. "Shinier."

I've thought about that many times since. No matter how

brightly we shine for him, we're still just reflecting his light. He will always shine brighter, because he's the source, the Morning Star, the star that rises first in our hearts, heralding the coming dawn.

Lord, help me rekindle a childlike faith in you
by paying close attention to my own children,
teaching them not only the words,
but also the meaning of
"Morning Star, O Cheering Sight!"

THE BEST MEDICINE

A merry heart does good, like medicine,
But a broken spirit dries the bones.

—PROVERBS 17:22

Don't feel like exercising today?

I have the perfect alternative for you: laughter.

Fifteen facial muscles get involved when we laugh, which is why after a good bout of laughter your cheeks hurt. That's your face's way of telling you, "Please do this more often!" You know the dangers of being a weekend jogger. The same thing happens when we don't exercise those facial muscles often enough.

Laughter makes us feel wonderful all over. Andrea from Pennsylvania concurs: "It feels so good to laugh. Just like the good feeling after exercising but with less work." Donna from Virginia confesses laughing is "the only exercise my body gets," and Jackie from Colorado insists it's "impossible to live without it. Like oxygen, food, God."

Sustenance indeed.

Was life meant to be fun? Of course. Not every minute of every day, but we should be laughing often enough that it won't hurt when we chuckle. Of all the muscles we're given to work with, our laugh muscles should be kept in the best shape possible. (And don't you love those workouts!)

The medical community and the spiritual community are (surprise) in agreement about the value of laughter. Doctors are known to keep lists of strange words and phrases that patients have used to describe their ills: migrating headaches, prospect glands, abstract teeth, and hideous hernias. One patient wanted a scat can of his brain, and another sought a better remedy than what he'd been using for muscle pain: Soybean, Jr.

You were hoping that I'd tell you laughing is aerobic, yes? It's true. Air is definitely involved. Scientists have proven you can exhale up to seventy-five miles an hour with a big laugh. WARNING: Better not sit in front of someone with false teeth.

To laugh out, you gotta breathe in, which qualifies as aerobic to me. I'm not sure you could sustain twenty minutes of laughter at your target heart rate three times a week . . . but think how delightful it would be to try!

Lord, when I grow sick of life and all its challenges,
remind me to take my merry medicine,
then share the prescription with others.
Laughter is the spoonful of tonic
our world so desperately needs right now.
Help us open our mouths wide, Lord . . .
and laugh!

PLAYING FOOTSY

How beautiful upon the mountains
Are the feet of him who brings good news . . .

—ISAIAH 52:7

When my feet are carrying the good news of the gospel, it doesn't matter what they look like. But, to be on the safe side, I'm keeping my shoes on.

Children's feet, at least, are soft and precious and small.

The feet of us big people are . . . well, big. Bony and gnarled. The word *cute* doesn't even come to mind.

There are three things nobody told me about The Maturing Foot:

1. Your feet may expand during pregnancy . . . and never go back.

I drove to the hospital wearing an 8½ shoe and came home wearing a 10B. I was prepared for my old clothes not to fit, but my *shoes?* The swollen ankles of my pregnancy receded, and I soon found out where the water went: right into my heels and toes.

Imagine disposing of an entire closet floor full of shoes, some so new they hadn't been worn yet. The worst part was having Bill watch me pull box after box out of the closet. He'd never seen the entire collection at a whack like that. "Who needs five pairs of black shoes?" he whined in exasperation.

We do, of course. Black flats for everyday wear, plain black pumps for work, black patent leather heels for Sundays, black high heels with bows for evening wear, and black loafers for . . . loafing. Hey, I figured they'd last me for years. How did I know my feet would grow in my late thirties? My earlobes, maybe, but my feet?

2. High heels will have less appeal.

When I tossed out all the shoes in my closet, I noticed an interesting phenomenon: The shoes that disappeared had two-inch heels; the new shoes that replaced them had one-inchers, max. When those wore out, the next generation had almost no heels at all. Now I'm wearing what amount to ballet shoes with rubber soles.

High heels are for younger women whose ankles still bend without breaking and whose fashion sense demands that elevated look. Out of respect for the gravity that is slowly but surely pulling me downward, I have chosen to retire my tippy-toe shoes for good. I think Job's friends were right: "A trap seizes him by the heel; / a snare holds him fast."[34] I am ensnared no more.

Flats are also fashionable again—still—and I think I know why. The designers couldn't bear watching us trot to work in their pricey outfits paired with huge neon-striped running shoes. That's why they designed high heels that were supposed to be as comfortable as sneakers and showed grown women playing basketball in them to prove it.

Nice try. Give us our flats, and we'll go away quietly.

3. The changes won't stop at your anklebone.

Here's another fine mess my body has gotten me into. I now have red blotches around my ankles. If I wear bobby sox, you can't see them, so with just the right length skirt (well below the knees) and properly positioned socks, my legs still look youthful in some lighting situations. Twilight for instance.

Many of us have quietly done away with panty hose in favor of an updated old favorite: knee-highs. Not only the cable-knit numbers in the winter, but the sheer-to-the-toe variety in warmer weather. They're a natural with slacks, but lots of us get away with them under dresses as well. WARNING: Your dress needs to be almost ankle length to pull this off without anyone knowing you're "cheating." One stiff breeze and we'll see your knees!

Fact is, it's getting harder to see your feet anyway as you age, right? Who cares if they're a tad wider, or your shoes are flatter, or your hose start at your knees? If you can put one foot in front of the other and keep moving, you're one lucky dame.

My feet may not be as adorable as they once were, Lord.
But I'm thrilled to know, when they're in your service,
my feet are still beautiful to you.
Help me celebrate the fact that I can still walk
and not fret over the shape or shade of my tootsies.

GO TO THE HEAD
OF THE CLASS

Rabbi, we know that You are a teacher come from God;
for no one can do these signs that You do unless God is with him.

—JOHN 3:2

His friends call him "Rabbi" because he spent twelve years in college—full-time—earning a Ph.D. in Old Testament Languages. I just call him my husband, Bill.

It's only fitting that I married a man whose many skills include teaching because I come from a whole family of teachers. My brother Dave calls it the "family business." Both my sisters are teachers, all three of my sisters-in-law have been teachers, two of my brothers are teachers . . . you get the idea.

I'm the black sheep of the family because I did not choose education as my career, and for good reason. It looked too much like work. Papers to grade in the evening, projects to build on the weekends, summer classes to earn a master's degree. Definitely work.

One August, when another school year loomed on the horizon, I asked teachers around the country, "What's the most frustrating thing about teaching?" Their answers can be summed up in three statements:

1. *Students who have no interest in learning*
2. *Bureaucratic chores*
3. *Lack of discipline and respect*

Jesus—our Rabbi, our Teacher—would understand. Among the crowds that came to hear him teach were many would-be students who had no interest in spiritual things and refused to listen, let alone follow. As to bureaucratic hassles, try dealing with the Sanhedrin. Respect? He was crucified for what he taught and who he was.

Yet, teach he did. Jesus taught with stories, with humor, with examples, with signs and wonders, with facts, with feelings, with every educational tool at his command.

Sometimes people really listened: "And so it was, when Jesus had ended these sayings, that the people were astonished at His teaching, for He taught them as one having authority, and not as the scribes."[35]

What does it mean, to teach with "authority"? Use a loud voice? Threaten bodily harm? Wave a big stick? No, teaching with authority means getting people to *do* what you teach them.

If you've ever taught a group of students, in any capacity, imagine if they actually *did* everything you asked them to do—the first time. Whoa.

Jesus taught his disciples by giving them tasks to do: "Go to this city," or "Find a man with a donkey." When his pupils obeyed, they invariably learned something about life, about themselves, and about the Lord they served.

We can still sit in his classroom this very day. With his textbook
—the Word of God—in our hands and our tutor—the Holy Spirit—
by our side, we can learn from the best Teacher this world has ever
seen.

Teach me, Lord.
I promise to listen. And obey.
Help me acknowledge your authority in my life
and do what you've asked me to do.
The first time.

Growth Spurts

Let the little children come to Me, and do not forbid them;
for of such is the kingdom of God.

—Mark 10:14

Whenever we visit family members, they marvel at our children and exclaim, "My, how they've grown!" Let's face it, that's what kids do best.

We parental types have grown right along with them. Our kids have taught us how to help another person blow his nose (no easy trick, this), how to eat sparingly (only brown food is edible), how hard it is to tie shoelaces upside down and backward, and how meaningful a hug is when you really love the huggee.

Children are also full of questions. "Why is the sky blue?" can be answered scientifically. "How many numbers are there?" can be answered mathematically.

But "Where does a gerbil go when it dies?" is a toughie. "Into the ground" is a cop-out. "Dust to dust" is too scary a scenario, and spinning tales of "gerbil heaven" is bad theology.

When Mrs. Gerbil breathed her last at our house, we had a good cry—all four of us. Lillian leaked first, of course, which set me off, which put Matthew under. When Bill returned from the burial mound, he found us all in a heap around the kitchen table and joined right in.

Some things are easy to explain. Other truths, as Bill would say, "aren't nailed down." Come to think of it, I've known some people who weren't all nailed down either. It may be those "loose boards" among us who can hit the nail on the head when it comes to answering life's toughest questions, especially if we answer truthfully: "Lord knows, child. Go ask your Father."

Three-year-old Larry asked his daddy a question and got more than he bargained for. The little boy was playing with Lego plastic building blocks on the floor when he looked up at his father and innocently asked, "How do you make babies?"

His dad took a deep breath and plunged in, explaining that babies are a gift from God and that the mommy and daddy pray for a baby and God answers those prayers.

Larry patiently waited for him to finish. Finally he sighed, "No, Daddy. How do you make babies out of Legos?"

Sometimes kids have answers to questions their fathers never even considered.

Rodney and his older sister Frances were playing outside in their bare feet one summer night. When bedtime rolled around, their father told Rodney to scrub his feet before he climbed under the covers. "Those feet are filthy!" his dad insisted.

A few minutes later, Rodney showed up for inspection. "How do they look?" he wanted to know.

"Fine, son, but you're going to get your feet dirty all over again by walking around without your slippers."

"No problem," Rodney assured him. "I didn't wash the bottoms."

Tee-hee. Have a good day, sis (whether you wash the bottoms or not . . . !).

> *Help me have the honest faith of a child, Lord,*
> *unafraid to ask the hard questions*
> *and willing to confess the truth,*
> *even if it costs me a spanking.*

Birds of a Feather

Look at the birds of the air, for they neither sow nor reap
nor gather into barns; yet your heavenly Father feeds them.
Are you not of more value than they?

—*Matthew 6:26*

How do you measure your value? Dollars in the bank? Cars in the driveway? Letters after your name? During the Depression, you were someone special if you had a little meat on your bones. That meant you were prosperous, that nobody at *your* house was starving. People could see you were well cared for. And for that matter, cared about.

Well, suppose we look at the birds of the air, as Jesus suggested. With rare exceptions they appear to be plump and healthy and flying high. Even though they have no food stored up for tomorrow, they seem to be doing fine today on the food that their heavenly Father has provided. Come to think of it, Jesus did pray, "Give us today our daily bread."[36] And he said we are of *more* value to God than those happily fed birds, meaning he will look out for *all* our needs—not only physical but spiritual needs as well.

Driving up the Pikes Peak Highway one summer, my family and I got a bird's-eye view of beautiful Colorado Springs. As the world below got smaller and smaller, I said to my children, "Wow! This is what we must look like to God!"

That was *not* the right thing to say.

Lillian started whimpering, and Matthew said, "But, Mom, we can't even *see* any people!"

Come to think of it, it *is* amazing that God can dwell in heaven yet see all the way inside our thick-skinned hearts. We really must be valuable for him to go to all that trouble.

Being valuable doesn't mean being treated like a precious gem, kept in a velvet-lined box and seldom worn. I once saw a sign posted in a local church: *Short Sermons, Cool Air, Warm Welcome.* A little too much velvet lining there.

No, being valuable means being vulnerable, flying through life without a safety net, knowing that God will provide everything we truly need.

Lord, there are days when I feel
of such little value
to myself or to my family.
To know that you find me valuable,
not because of what I do
but simply because I'm yours,
is even more delicious than my daily bread.

REAL JOY

But I will sing of Your power;
Yes, I will sing aloud of Your mercy in the morning.

—PSALM 59:16A

Is your stereo already on this morning, sis? Mine, too. I love music at any hour, especially when the notes are aimed heavenward.

It was Saturday night at a women's retreat in Michigan. Several hundred of us were having some serious fun, singing praise songs and listening to a woman named Robin play classical music with such passion that it brought tears to our eyes. The grand piano was practically lifting off the stage when her hands hit the keyboard for the final chords. *Bong! Bong! Ba-bong!* We were breathless as we applauded wildly.

But Robin had more up her sleeve.

Her hands began to dance across the black-and-whites, her ample bottom began to dance across the padded bench, and our hearts began to dance in our rib cages as this holy woman, this former nun, started playing sanctified *boogie-woogie* with a right-eous rhythm!

We were standing by this point. We were moving. Swaying. Before the night was over, we'd learned how to worship not only with all our hearts but with our feet too. In the bargain, we'd learned the macarena!

Robin says she's fifty-five, but don't you believe it. In her heart, she is a child again, set free with the discovery that when you give all of who you are to the One you love—every gift, every flaw, every facet of your personality—you are free to experience Real Joy.

She radiated Real Joy that night. We experienced Real Joy just by being there. When I spoke to the same crowd the next morning, I threw out my notes (trust me, this is not my usual style!) and spoke from the heart about the healing power of laughter and the freeing power of giving everything to God and letting go of the outcome. I have never had more fun on the platform, and I've never seen an audience laugh harder. Why? Robin showed us all how to let go and let God.

I stumbled upon a big "aha" that weekend. Instead of looking at younger women and wishing I had their carefree lifestyle and thin thighs, I found myself watching an older woman, wishing I could be more like her. *Yes!*

This is Real Joy: knowing that "To everything there is a season, / A time for every purpose under heaven."[37] This is our season, babe. Let's not waste a minute wishing it were otherwise. We have too much laughing, too much dancing, too much singing to do.

Joy unspeakable, Lord—
that's what it means to grow in the knowledge of you.
May the music of my heart and the praise of my lips
celebrate you through every season of my life.

Healing Power

Happy are the people who are in such a state;
Happy are the people whose God is the LORD!

—PSALM 144:15

Are you feeling less than happy this morning because some physical challenge has robbed you of joy? Be encouraged, dear one. Laughter is still possible. Those who have survived cancer never fail to praise the benefits of maintaining, even enhancing, one's sense of humor through the recovery process.

Karleen from Indiana shares, "My daughter had just undergone surgery for ovarian cancer for the second time, and upon returning to her room, she found several of us waiting for her, including her husband, Robert."

"Oh, Robert," her daughter said, "don't look so sad. I'm going to be all right. God put me in your life to make you miserable, and I'm not through yet!"

What a testimony to this woman's faith, strength, and ability to overcome adversity with humor. Phyllis from Michigan says, "I truly believe laughter is God's pain medicine for the hurts of life. No matter what valley we go through, God provides a way to rejoice in him always, and sometimes that's through laughter."

Humor is by no means the only positive emotional experience that promotes healing. Love and affection make all the difference in the world—the love of God and the love of people you care about. Faith and hope walk beside love and laughter, as do a patient's will to live and the unique calling that gives his or her life meaning. There is great comfort to be found in glorious music, delicious scents, the beauty of nature, and the warmth of light.

Laughter weaves its carefree way through all those joy-filled, purpose-filled, spirit-filled blessings. We humans are a complex bunch. Only God, who knows us and loves us completely, has the power to meet our needs and bless our lives in so personal a way that we feel he is ministering to us alone.

The one who knows God can laugh in the face of death because to die with Christ in your heart is to live—and laugh—with him, forever.

Lord, I release to you my fear of disease, my dread of death.
If I am well this day, let me give you all the credit for it.
If my body is less than healthy, let me lean on you completely,
trusting my flesh and spirit to your loving care.
Thank you that someday I will stand in your heavenly presence,
healthy and whole, forever.

BUILDING A TRUST FUND

The heart of her husband safely trusts her.

—Proverbs 31:11

Let's face it: You can fall in love, but you can't fall in trust. Trust doesn't come from romantic dinners and kisses on the doorstep. Trust, unlike love, is not blind. Trust is based on time, experience, and year-in, year-out faithfulness. It takes a few turns of the calendar before "her husband has full confidence in her."[38]

After many years of marriage, I can say with assurance that Bill and I trust each other completely. He trusts me with our money, the mutual care of our children, and all our possessions, even the riding lawn mower and the remote control. Most of all, he trusts me with his *heart,* his emotional center. As his best friend, I know all his tender spots, pressure points, and fault lines, and I keep them well guarded.

Love and trust walk hand in hand. When a group of girlfriends gathered with me to study Proverbs 31 one summer, I gave them a homework assignment: "Ask your husband, 'What speaks love to you?' Don't worry, he'll know what you mean." They came back with their research, and we found the answers to be very different than we'd expected. One husband said he sensed his wife's love for him "by the look in your eyes when I enter the room"; another mentioned, "the way you address me in conversation"; a third answered, "the sacrifices you are willing to make on our behalf." With answers like that, it's a question worth asking.

In our marriage, Bill poses a particular question several times a week. He knows just when I need to hear it—when my to-do list is on tilt and I'm feeling overwhelmed. Bill simply says, "What can I do to bless you tonight?" And he means specific tasks, something he could do to make my life easier—the dishes, the laundry, the groceries, whatever.

Do I deserve a man this good? Absolutely not. But I don't deserve grace either, and I'm grateful to have that poured over me daily.

Lord, let me be worthy of my husband's trust
and ever grateful for the many practical blessings
he bestows on me.
Nudge me daily to find ways to bless him back,
and let me guard his tender heart
as a treasure,
a gift entrusted to me by you.

Balance and Grace

Let us therefore come boldly to the throne of grace,
that we may obtain mercy and find grace to help in time of need.

—Hebrews 4:16

What does this day hold for you, dear one?

Too much to do in too little time? Too many people with too many demands?

Or perhaps you (like me) are your own worst taskmaster, expecting too much from yourself in any given twenty-four hours.

Today is the day, then, to seek balance. And grace. The more difficult the season of our lives, the more balance and grace we need to see it through.

Bill and I often send each other greeting cards, not just for the usual occasions but sometimes just because. One especially stressful and unbalanced week, his card included this encouraging notation: "It's been a long, hard day, and for that matter a long, hard week (for that matter, a long, hard year!!). I love you, Liz, and want to help you find a lifestyle that is fulfilling to you and yet practical for all of us. Let me love you through this tough time."

I did. I do. I always will, sweet Bill.

As a couple, we continue to discuss, adjust, negotiate, and

hammer out a lifestyle that seeks to honor God, his Word, and our own abilities and desires. By staying in tune and in touch with each other, we try to keep the guilt meter on low and the grace meter on high.

As a wife, mother, writer, and speaker, I long to feel that at each given moment I'm walking in God's perfect will for my life. And so I pray. And listen. And look to the Lord for guidance wherever I walk and for grace whenever I stumble, resting in the truth that "God created complexity. It's okay not to have all the answers."[39]

What a relief! Because I don't have all the answers. Sometimes I'm not even sure I'm asking the right questions. I simply focus on serving God, loving people, and doing my best to make a difference in my own spheres of influence. It's not necessary to do more. And it's not satisfying to do less.

Lord, how we wish we really could "do it all,"
that we could have our lives in perfect order,
balanced and harmonious.
Everything in tune,
all things accomplished.
The house, the job, the hubby, the kids,
the church, the school, the friends and neighbors,
the organizations, the expectations.
Lord, I get weary even thinking of it all.
Give me the wisdom and grace
to know when to say yes and where to say no.

BOUGHT WITH A PRICE

Fear not, for I have redeemed you;
I have called you by your name;
You are Mine.

—ISAIAH 43:1B

If you're headed to the grocery store today, my friend, don't forget to clip those coupons—who doesn't like to save money?

Redeeming a coupon is a simple process if you follow the rules. You have to purchase the correct item—the right brand, the right size box, the right flavor, the right weight to the ounce—and you have to do so before the expiration date, or the whole thing is null and void. Cashiers are carefully trained coupon readers, so nothing gets past them. Nothing.

Once you follow the rules, though, they subtract the amount of the coupon from the price of your item. They can't add any new restrictions or say, "Come back tomorrow," or "Sorry, we changed our mind." No, if you follow the rules, the redemption is complete and you walk out with your discount, which amounts to cash in your pocket.

You, too, have been redeemed—but not with a piece of paper clipped out of *Good Housekeeping*. No, you've been redeemed with the blood of Jesus Christ, shed for you on the cross. He, too, had to follow the rules, laid down centuries earlier by his heavenly father. The rules of redemption said that, apart from the shedding of blood, there was no forgiveness of sin. Furthermore, the sacrifice had to be perfect, which meant one alone could serve as Redeemer: God himself.

I wonder why God made such a demanding set of rules in the first place, knowing where it would lead. Who needs rules, anyway?

We do.

Our son, Matthew, was eager to play a new board game, but when he got it all set up, he realized the printed rules of the game were nowhere to be found. After searching in all the obvious places, he said with a shrug, "Let's just roll the dice."

He moved ahead three spaces; I moved ahead five. Now what? We didn't know why the squares were different colors or what we were supposed to do when we landed in Crocodile Creek. We rolled again and kept moving around the board, but it quickly became more frustrating than fun. We tried making up some rules, awarding points for even numbers and subtracting them for odd, but we couldn't remember the rules from one turn to the next. Soon we gave up and started an all-out search for the missing instructions.

We need rules. Otherwise we'll never finish the game, let alone know whether we won or lost. Jesus knew the rules when he came to earth, and he played by them even though it meant the most painful, humiliating death one could imagine. The rules said that the innocent must die for the guilty, the perfect for the imperfect, the one for the many.

On redemption day, Jesus walked in prepared to follow all the rules. He paid the price. He bought you back and considered it worth the terrible cost. How he values your soul, my sister!

The price you paid for my redemption is beyond comprehension.
You followed the rules, even though I broke them.
Because of your sacrifice, Lord, I'm redeemed...
how I love to proclaim it!

Have You Any Wool?

For you were like sheep going astray,
but have now returned to
the Shepherd and Overseer of your souls.

—1 Peter 2:25

As a woman who lives in a nineteenth-century farmhouse and loves the country look in decorating, I've always thought sheep were cute. After all, the ones I usually see at craft fairs are made of pure white fluffy wool with round wooden legs and little button eyes. They cost about $34.95, unless you want a full-size model for $59.95. I've never succumbed (bad stewardship), but I do think they're sweet looking.

The real problem is, they in no way resemble real sheep.

Real sheep are (dare I say it?) not as cosmetically appealing. Some of them have strange, piercing eyes, positioned so close together as to make them look cross-eyed. None of them are anywhere near as white as the kind in the store. They've got stuff hanging all over them, from food to worse, and consequently they don't smell very nice either, even on a cool breezy day. In the heat of summer, baby, look out!

That's not to say that sheep aren't lovable. By no means. They have so many needs and are so dependent on their shepherd, you can't help but want to take care of them. And they need a lot of care, because—please don't think I'm being cruel when I say this—sheep are definitely *stupid*.

They will eat grass until they get to the roots, then eat the roots so grass will never grow back, and then bleat about, wondering where the grass went, when all the while delicious green grass is ten feet away.

They also can be "cast down," which means they get in a comfy little spot and stretch just so and suddenly they're on their backs with all four of their little feet up in the air, and they are *stuck*. Surely It was a sheep that first bleated, "Help, I've fallen, and I can't get up!" *Bleat. Bleat.*

Enter a kind shepherd who hears the bleating, finds the sheep, and helps the animal back on its feet. Because if it's left that way, the sheep is doomed, and it's at least smart enough to know that much.

So you see, when Jesus said that we are like sheep, this was not a compliment. He clearly stated that we're not as intelligent as we think we are, nor do we know what's best for us, nor can we keep ourselves out of danger. You can't even think of the word *sheep* in Scripture without also thinking of the words *going astray*. They are also creatures of habit and stubborn to boot. Is that us, or what?

Here's the happy ending: We have a Shepherd who loves us, knows us, cares deeply for us, watches over us, looks out for us, keeps his staff on hand to lift us out of danger. He feeds us from his rich pastures, he leads us to still waters, he restores our souls.

What a Shepherd!

Lord, I'm grateful that you watch over your flocks
day and night.
Help me stay close to your side
and bleat for help rather than go astray.

Transformed
by Grace

But we all, with unveiled face, beholding as in a mirror
the glory of the Lord, are being transformed into the same image
from glory to glory, just as by the Spirit of the Lord.

—*2 Corinthians 3:18*

Come with me to my dining room several houses ago. It was a room I never spent much time in because, frankly, I am cooking impaired. Few friends of mine would ever say, "Oh, boy! Let's go to Liz's house for dinner."

Nonetheless, when I invited these two dear women from work to come to my church, then join me at my house for Sunday dinner, they said yes right away. Taste impaired, it seemed, and I was grateful for it.

The church service was especially meaningful that day. Seated between my two friends, one a new believer in Christ, the other a seeker who had not quite taken "the big leap," I spent most of the worship hour praying like mad for both of them to move forward in their faith. As a fairly new believer, I didn't have all the answers to their questions, but I did have *the* answer—Jesus—and told them everything I knew about him.

Heading to my house after church, we had a lively discussion about the message and the music, since both were different in style from their own experiences in church growing up. The conversation continued as I prepared dinner (such as it was) and put our food on the table.

There we were, in the middle of serving the vegetables, when my new sister in faith blurted out, "Hey, have you ever seen that poster called 'Footprints'?"

My pseudointellectual siren went off in my head. *Oh, brother, what a corny message that is. Everybody knows about "Footprints." You can get it on a key chain, for heaven's sake.*

Maybe so. But our seeking friend had never heard of it.

And so my dear sister, full of enthusiasm for her newfound Savior, shared the story of the set of footprints in the sand—first two sets, then one. Big, beautiful tears were rolling down her cheeks. "Don't you see? God carried him! That's why there was just one set of prints."

I was teary-eyed by this point, too, but was surprised to see my other guest also had wet cheeks.

That was nothing compared to what happened next.

She reached out for both our hands and bowed her head, her lovely dark hair just inches from my pitiful green bean casserole. "God," she said, her voice shaking with emotion, "I know you've been carrying me all along. Please let me be a Christian like my friends."

I am crying again, right now, as I put these words on paper. I was a witness to the transforming power of Jesus Christ, live and in person, a soul delivered from darkness to light, right there in my jade green dining room!

Dinner was forgotten. We jumped up and hugged the breath out of each other. We laughed until we cried and cried until we laughed. I put my favorite song of the hour, "More Than Wonderful," on the stereo, and we sang it at full volume, without knowing the words.

In the midst of this joyful celebration, our brand-new sister in Christ saw a camera sitting on the counter. "Oh, Liz, please take a picture of me. I think I even *look* different!"

Indeed she did. The transformation had begun.

That photo, which I kept on my refrigerator for years, captures the whole message of grace in one glorious, beautiful, shining face.

Now it's your turn, sis.

Look closely in your mirror. Can you see her, looking back at you?

Will you let the Lord transform you so completely that when people see you, they'll say, "You look terrific! What's different?"

You are!

What a day that was, Lord!
Bless you for letting me
see for myself
the transforming power of forgiveness.
Not only in her heart, Lord,
but also in her face . . . amazing, that grace!
There's another woman on my heart.
The one holding this book.
She really matters to me, Lord.
May her face shine with the
light of knowing you.

You Gotta Have Friends

A friend is always loyal,
and a brother is born to help in time of need.

—*Proverbs 17:17* NLT

Friend (noun): Someone who cries when you cry, laughs when you laugh, tells you when you have lipstick on your teeth or a run in your panty hose, and never tells a soul your age or dress size.

That's not the Webster definition, babe; that's the Lizzie Revised Version.

My friends over the years have stuck with me through thick and thin (thick, mostly). I love when they have a little fun at my expense. It means they love me and know our friendship is secure enough to handle it. As Janet sees it, "At age 6, presents are important; at 60, it's who brings them."

In high school our friends applied peer pressure. In later years they apply zero pressure. You can disagree with an adult friend and not worry about losing his vote for senior class secretary. You can cry on a friend's shoulder and know she won't think you're weird (just menopausal). Friends may know how to "push your buttons" by the time you've reached adulthood, but they also know how to soothe your hurts and help you get back on track.

Imagine being part of a bunco club like Patricia's, which has had the same members and same meeting date for the past *twenty-nine years.* "We started as young brides—newly married, thin, full of hopes and dreams, and seeing life through rose-colored glasses. As the years have passed, our rose-colored glasses have turned into prescription bifocals. The brides and grooms in our lives are now our children, and we still have hopes and dreams of being able to sleep all night and not hear a door open or telephone ring. We have learned about clothes that shrink in the closet and how signs have become smaller."

Much smaller. Minuscule, even.

"When we share our pictures of grandchildren, we also have to share our glasses. We've also given up on playing bunco—we couldn't keep track of the dice and the conversation at the same time—and instead have what we jokingly call our group therapy sessions. Does it save us money! I've learned that no matter how successful one is or how much money one makes, life would be very empty without our friends."

Preach it, Patricia.

So, who are *your* three closest friends? Find a way to contact them—today—and tell them they fill your life to the brim.

Lord, I'm so grateful for my earthly friends.
Each one fills my cup to overflowing.
Yet it's you, Lord, who are my
best friend of all.

Split Ends

If we are faithless, He remains faithful;
He cannot deny Himself.

—2 Timothy 2:13

Some people are fickle when it comes to things like haircuts and manicures.

Not me, girlfriend. I am faithful, through and through.

I've known Carol, my hairstylist, longer than I've known my husband. Our paths crossed in 1984, and I've faithfully sat in her chair ever since. When Carol switched salons, I followed her across town. "Whither thou goest, I will go," I assured her.

Who wouldn't declare lifelong loyalty to someone who combines amateur therapist skills with the latest techniques in blunt cutting? Carol patiently listened through my career and dating woes, nodding sympathetically as her scissors snipped away. Those were the perm years—natural color, unnatural curl. Then when hubby-to-be Bill came into my life, Carol and I dumped the perm in favor of longer locks to please my sweetie. Months later, it was Carol who styled the tresses of my wedding party, and Carol again who gave me a pedicure the week before my first child was slated to arrive, so I'd have fashionable toes in the delivery room.

Talk about a labor of love!

Our relationship isn't one-sided, either. I sang at Carol's wedding and rejoiced when she began taking college courses at night. We've laughed, cried, and compared notes on husbands, kids, and cleaning services. You can't simply walk away from that kind of dual commitment over something as frivolous as a few frizzy perms or doubtful dye jobs.

Carol and I are friends. Girl buddies. Partners in the fight against dark roots and stray chin hairs. Who could say "Sayonara" to a soul sister like that?

Hard to believe how frighteningly close I came to committing hair-care infidelity. Just the memory of it makes my scalp itch. I was having my photo taken, and arrangements were made for my makeup and hair. After the cosmetician did a bang-up job on eyes, lips, and cheeks, it was time to put my hair in the hands of a stranger.

Steve the Stylist rested his hands lightly on my shoulders, and my stomach tightened. I felt like a nervous teenager on a first date.

"Is there a particular way you'd like me to style your hair?"

Yes, I wanted to say, *Carol's way!* Instead, I gulped, "Nooo, just make me look ten pounds thinner, and I'll be happy."

His graceful hands danced around my head, comb in one hand, industrial-strength hair spray in the other. I watched in amazement. I was getting thinner! Wow, Carol never parted it like that. How did he do that lift-and-poof thing on the side? Fascinating.

Steve finally whipped off my plastic cape with a flourish. "There you are, Liz. What do you think?"

I think I'm in love. No, no, not with you—just your hands. Are you this good with scissors? Know your way around a bottle of peroxide?

I realized the dangerous direction my imagination was taking me and mentally swatted away the little voices taunting me: *He's the one! He's the one! Leave Carol and cleave to Steve!*

When Steve slipped me his business card and suggested I give him a call sometime, I stuffed it in my pocket, mumbled a red-faced "thank you," and hotfooted it for the door.

I knew I should have tossed that card in the circular file, but I couldn't resist tucking it in my Rolodex, "just in case." In case Carol moved away or quit the business. Or was eaten by sharks. Otherwise, I would not defect to Steve. Would not, could not.

But my fingers kept flipping past his name. Would Carol notice if I did one little color weave with Steve? Maybe a teensy trim, between real haircuts? If I timed it right, she'd never be the wiser. I reached for the phone and dialed Steve's salon. The receptionist was sharp, cool, professional. Yes, Steve had an opening on Tuesday. A weave? Of course, no problem, two o'clock is fine. See you then, Mrs. Higgs.

I almost slammed the phone down. *What was I thinking?* As the calendar marched toward Tuesday, I spent more time on my hair than usual, trying to convince myself to undo my risk-filled liaison. *It's not that bad a cut,* I told myself. *In fact, it's a very good cut or Steve couldn't have styled it so nicely.*

Tuesday morning dawned gray and menacing. Cowardice leaped from my heart and into my fingers as I dialed the Other

Salon's number and canceled my appointment, muttering a feeble excuse about my too-full schedule.

I waited for my racing heart to slow back down to normal, then hit the speed-dial button that instantly put me in touch with my regular salon. *My* salon, Carol's salon. Home.

"A cut with Carol at two o'clock? No problem, Liz. See you then. Hug the kids for me."

I hung up the phone in blessed relief, tossing Steve's card in the wastebasket. No more flirting with temptation; I'd stick with a place where everybody knows my name.

Especially Carol.

You spared me, Lord, from undoing
a long-term friendship that goes much deeper
than the roots of my hair.
How quickly we toss aside relationships
when the grass looks greener next door.
I confess I've done my share of church hopping
for the same fickle, foolish reason:
hoping for something better.
Help me honor you by
remaining true to my friends,
loyal to my commitments,
and faithful to your body, the Church.

THE BEST OF INTENTIONS

She does him good and not evil
All the days of her life.

—*PROVERBS 31:12*

One problem here: This verse doesn't leave any room for "she puts up with him!" She not only does *not* do her man evil, but she does only good things. That's a lot of pressure for us less-than-angelic wives who try hard but stumble, even as we try to "comfort, encourage and do him only good."[40]

If your reaction is, "How come he doesn't have to be good to *me?*" don't worry. He does. There are plenty of verses that point to the quality of the marriage relationship, the concept of serving one another, belonging to one another, etc. Meanwhile, doing good rather than evil to the men we love just makes sense.

My husband has the patience of Job. If we're sitting at a red light, and he's behind the wheel, I'm over on the passenger's side with an invisible gas pedal of my own. I stretch my foot toward it as I crane my neck to the left and right, ready to take off like a shot.

The light changes. Bill's foot is still on the brake.

"Bill, it's green!" I say, assuming he just didn't see it change.

Still no forward motion. He's looking around, hands positioned on the wheel at 10:00 and at 2:00.

Desperation mounts. "Bill, it's green!"

He turns to me and says, "There'll be another one."

I'm the first to admit that I often have a little fun at Bill's expense, but there are two important considerations: First, I run every story past him before I use it on the platform or in my writing. If he seems the least bit hurt, it's history, though most of the time he loves it and adds another funny line or two of his own. Second, I make certain that for every one of those good-natured ribbings, I share two kinder comments about him.

Women are so used to male-bashing humor that I find the more I praise Bill in public, the more women come up to me afterward, conviction on their faces. "Listening to you, Liz, I've realized that I never say positive things about my husband. That's going to change as of tonight."

You go, girl.

We know this truth from experience: To do "good and not evil" to the man we love is not only the right thing, it's the smart thing. Sooner or later, those kind words and deeds just might head back in our direction.

> *Lord, remind me that loving my husband*
> *is just like loving you.*
> *It's an act of worship.*
> *And an act of obedience.*

Let me speak well of him,

even in jest.

Let me do him good,

whether he deserves it or not.

Because that's how you treat me, Lord Jesus.

Roots and Fruits

He shall be like a tree
Planted by the rivers of water,
That brings forth its fruit in its season,
Whose leaf also shall not wither;
And whatever he does shall prosper.

—PSALM 1:3

Any farmer will tell you that fruit trees take time and effort to grow. You prepare the soil, plant them with care, and then you wait.

Wait while the tree digs its roots down deep in the nutrient-rich soil, searching for fresh rivers of water. Wait some more while it stretches its branches toward the light of the sun and a refreshing breeze. Still more waiting, while the sapling finds its place in the delicately balanced environment.

Then, as surely as winter turns to spring, the tree silently brings forth fruit in its season. It may take a year, or two, or three, but the fruit does appear without any struggle on the part of the tree. I've never heard an apple tree groan in the moonlight, trying to make apples, have you? God brings forth the fruit because God made the tree. Simple botany.

The type of fruit is determined by the kind of tree it is; apple trees naturally make apples. Inside the fruit are seeds destined to create many more fruit-bearing trees, if the seeds are planted in good soil.

In the same way, you are also a tree in the kingdom of God. Some of us have bigger trunks than others, but we're all trees!

We dig our roots down deep in the soil of God's Word, seeking out the Living Water that only Christ can provide. We stretch our branches upward toward the Son and are refreshed by the *pneuma*, the wind of the Holy Spirit.

Most of the tree's work is done underground, quietly. No one keeps track. No one checks the roots. Your growth is sure, but slow. So slow that those around you may not notice your spiritual growth at first. But God sees it, right away.

Finally, when the branches of your tree are strong enough to support it, the fruit arrives in its season—no sooner, no later. What does the fruit of a believer look like? More new Christians, perhaps, thanks to your encouragement. Good works for God's glory, like food baskets and clothing drives for those in need. Delicious fruit indeed.

The process is simple: We grow the roots. God grows the fruits.

Lord, forgive me when I'm too busy checking for fruit
and not spending enough time digging my roots
deep into the rich soil of your Word.
Strengthen my branches
and toughen my bark.
And . . . send rain, Lord!

POT SCRUBBER

Therefore if anyone cleanses himself . . . he will be a
vessel for honor, sanctified and useful for the Master,
prepared for every good work.

—*2 Timothy 2:21*

No two ways about it, I was not "prepared for any good work" that
day. Bill and I had just had an unpleasant exchange in the car on
the way to my presentation—one for a precious gathering of sisters
in Christ, no less! Don't worry, there wasn't any screaming or curs-
ing going on in the front seat, but it *was* rather meanspirited.

Our argument ended in silence. A heavy stillness filled the air
with unspoken angst. Young Lillian, ever the intuitive one, asked,
"If you knew way back when you got married that it would be like
this, why did you do it?"

I felt as if I'd suddenly been nailed to the car seat. "Good question!" was my lippy retort, which I regretted instantly but could not
inhale back into my mouth. Instead, I took a deep breath, tried not
to look at Bill, and said as carefully as I could, "Lillian, even though
Mom and Dad disagree, it doesn't mean we don't love each other.
We do. Very much."

I thought this answer might serve double duty as an "I'm sorry" to Bill. But it didn't, of course, because there wasn't a repentant syllable in it.

By this time we'd reached the front of the hotel, and I bounded out of the car. My hostess greeted me, waved at Bill, and in I went, leaving him to find a parking space so the poor dear could unload my books. I'm lucky he didn't toss them out the window after me.

As the morning progressed, filled with wonderful music and warm greetings from the platform, it was my turn to be introduced. I smiled, I spoke, they laughed, all was well, except for one small problem: My vessel was clogged with the dirt of unconfessed sin. I knew it and God knew it and Bill knew it. True, the women seated before me didn't know it, but *I* knew.

Finally, I told them about the incident so they'd know too. Thankfully, they'd had one or two discussions along the same lines with their own husbands, so they understood. We laughed even more, but this time my own laughter had wings instead of weights. I couldn't wait to see Bill, ask his forgiveness, and clear up things between us.

A. W. Tozer said, "The Lord can use any vessel, even if it's cracked, as long as it's clean." My vessel is bigger than many and more cracked than most, but thanks to the cleansing blood of the Savior, it's washable.

> *Lord, I know I'm only useful to your kingdom*
> *when I'm free of the debris of unconfessed sin.*
> *Whatever it takes, Lord—*
> *the insight of a child or the harsh light of day—*
> *show me where I need to scrub a little harder.*

WRINKLES IN TIME

The boundary lines have fallen for me in pleasant places . . .

—PSALM 16:6 NIV

I make it a practice never to put on lipstick outdoors on a bright, sunny day. One glance in that mirror, and it's curtains for my confidence . . .

> *Wrinkles are one thing I've had to face,*
> *And they seem to turn up every place.*
> *In years long gone, they were only in clothes,*
> *But they've moved to my face, and Lord only knows*
> *Where else, on my person, wrinkles may be . . .*
> *There are so many places that I can't see!*
> *—Judith Huffman, 51*

Soon after my fortieth (how *did* they know?), I received an envelope in the mail filled with slick literature about a wrinkle-minimizing system. Not just a cream, not merely a moisturizer, this was all those and more: a *pill.* A pill "based on the work of a famed Scandinavian skin specialist" (who wasn't putting his/her name on *anything*). It was advertised as a "quantum leap in the war on wrinkles . . . works from the inside out!"

Well, I *am* working on my wrinkles from the inside out. My goal is to stay plump enough to keep those wrinkles nicely filled up and therefore save $154.85 on a three-month supply of their wrinkle-minimizing system. If you're going to spend $1.72 a day, why not just buy three jelly donuts? It would accomplish the same thing and be more fun.

So we have wrinkles, so what? Now that those pesky teenage blemishes are gone, we can use concealer all over our faces. Just don't make the same mistake I do of confusing the flesh-colored tube of concealer with my almost-identical tube of anti-feathering lipstick base. I end up with blemishes that don't feather and lips you can't see. But at least the wrinkles are minimized!

I long for the days when I could face the world *sans* makeup, when moisturizer was something you smoothed on your legs after a day in the sun, when Noxema and water kept you looking dewy fresh around the clock, and when your face didn't look like you slept in it.

Ah, but . . .

Wrinkles not only come from time and the sun but also from laughing at the absurdities of life, which increase exponentially as we mature. They come from looking surprised when your child hands you a woolly worm she found on the porch. They come from smiling when you see an old friend who is as wrinkled as you are. They are a road map of experiences that you alone have enjoyed.

I'm learning to embrace the psalmist's words about lines that fall "in pleasant places." Even if they have fallen on my face, at least I can keep track of them there, knowing every single wrinkle was earned with time well spent.

Wrinkles are one thing I'm glad to face, Lord.
They simply announce, "Been there!"
They're a badge of courage, a mark of maturity,
proof positive that I know what I'm talking about
when I say with confidence,
"Jesus Christ is the same
yesterday, today,
and forever."[41]

Fill 'Er Up

But encourage one another daily, as long as it is called Today,
so that none of you may be hardened by sin's deceitfulness.

—Hebrews 3:13 niv

In my early years of speaking, people would kindly ask, "What do you speak about?" I'd find myself stumbling around looking for some word that would describe a blend of humor and inspiration. One time I blurted out, "Well, I encourage people," and a woman said, "I get it. You're an encourager."

Bong!

It was truly an aha moment, divinely inspired. I loved it so much, I had it trademarked, just as it is on the cover of this book: *An Encourager®.*

The more I studied the word *encourage,* the more excited I got. For one thing, it's biblical. Joseph the Levite was better known as "Barnabas," meaning "Son of Encouragement." In some translations, encouragement shows up as a spiritual gift, right up there with preaching and teaching. Furthermore, the word *courage* is the French word for "heart." I love filling people's hearts as an encourager!

You can be one, too. Not as a registered trademark, but definitely as your heavenly calling. That's why I chose to be *an* encourager, not *the* encourager. The job is too big for one woman alone.

As encouragers we're called to exhort, beseech, comfort, console, strengthen, persuade, support, sustain, cheer, embolden, entreat, build up, appeal, urge, and invite . . . and that's just for starters. Join me as a "daughter of encouragement." I think our brother Barnabas would be grateful for the company.

> *Lord, our world is starving for*
> *genuine encouragement.*
> *The kind that fills the heart,*
> *rather than draining it.*
> *That builds up,*
> *rather than tears down.*
> *Fill my own heart, Jesus.*
> *Let it overflow in the direction*
> *where your encouragement is needed most.*

Mothering Is a Profession Too

And let us not grow weary while doing good,
for in due season we shall reap if we do not lose heart.

—Galatians 6:9

I try not to laugh out loud when I hear younger women say, "I'm going to stick with this job until I'm thirty, then quit working and have children."

"Don't worry." I smile sweetly. "You'll still be working."

As the T-shirt says, "Every Mother Is a Working Mother." We work in the home, out of the home, and around the home. Working is what we do, yes? No surprise, this: We were ushered into motherhood through a process called *labor!*

The challenge for many of us—maybe you, dear one?—is to give our best effort to mothering while we're home and give our all to working while we're elsewhere, without feeling we've short-changed one or the other—or both.

When the kids see my suitcase at the door or find me all dressed up in panty hose and heels, they know I'm off to give a speech (believe me, I don't wear panty hose unless absolutely necessary!).

Because I have such an excellent track record for returning home within a day or two, the children seldom display any misery about Mother's leaving.

In fact, for years they thought I spoke at the airport. After all, that's where their dad dropped me off and picked me up. I think they'd decided that I simply rode to the top of the escalator and spoke to anyone who would listen!

In the early years, when they saw the heels and hose, Matthew gave me his biggest, toothiest smile. "Mama, have a good speech!" (That enthusiasm has since waned with the teenage years, but I enjoyed every minute of it while it lasted.)

When I would land at the Louisville airport the next day and run into their waiting arms, guess what Matthew would ask me right away? "Mama, did you have a good speech?"

Now, what do you suppose I told that angel of a boy? "No way! I just showed up, put in my time, collected my check, and left." Obviously not. Matthew deserves better than that, and so do my audiences. And so does my Lord Jesus. My prayer is that when I come home, I can look my children in the eyes and say with a clear conscience, "Mama did her best."

Being a working-outside-of-the-home mother doesn't mean I give less than my best effort because I regret not being home. If anything, I long to make that time *count* for something, and I don't mean just dollars.

My high school drama coach always reminded us, "There are no small roles, only small actors." Whatever role God has given us to play out on the stage called Life, we need to stretch out our hands and grab the chalk, the telephone, the computer, the thermo-meter, the disposable diapers, the car seat, and go for it. Without apology. Without compromise. Without giving less than our best because our salary could be better or because we'd rather be somewhere else.

Our children, our husbands, our parents, our friends, our peers, and our Lord are in the audience . . . let's give 'em a show!

Lord Jesus, it's difficult to do both jobs well—
working and mothering.
Give me the energy I need to keep going
and the vision I need to see
why this work matters
to you, to my family, to others.
Help me not to grow weary,
nor to lose heart,
knowing that everything I do—
from running the vacuum
to running Lilly to Scouts
to running through airports—
counts for something
in your kingdom's economy.
I love having you
for my boss, Jesus.

Open Mouth, Insert Soap

Do not let any unwholesome talk come out of your mouths,
but only what is helpful for building others up according to their needs,
that it may benefit those who listen.

—EPHESIANS 4:29 NIV

Remember the movie *Look Who's Talking*? Maybe it should have been titled *"Look Who's Listening,"* because our kids spend the first decade of their lives taking in nearly every word we say (and the next decade ignoring us completely!).

In the first two years, they're listening to vowels and consonants and words so they can imitate us and say something we'll recognize: "Ma-ma!" Music to our ears. In the preschool years, they're listening for grammar and usage and sentence construction to make their needs known more clearly. Once in school, language becomes a means of getting an "A" with a star on your paper or getting a "D" with a lecture.

Words have the power to change our mood, change our thinking, change our lives. Which is why I am so disappointed in myself when I think of how often I open my mouth to criticize, gossip, make a catty remark, praise myself, speak in anger, or offer some unsupportive comment. Or just plain *yell*. Ugh.

It was Ben Franklin who said, "Anger is never without reason, but seldom with a good one." Lately it seems that many people live on the edge of anger, ready to explode at any moment. These are the ones who cut us off in traffic and make an ugly face at us to boot.

True confession, sis: I've played that part a few times myself. Having spent years immersed in the wild ways of the world, I'd developed a vocabulary that was . . . ah . . . *colorful.* Since I wanted to move past my past and avoid exposing my children to those particular shades of blue again, I made a list of "Ten Things I *Could* Say, if I *Would* Say, but I *Won't* Say."

Use your imagination.

On second thought, *don't!*

Then I gave each one of those words or phrases a number, one through ten.

When the urge to say something inappropriate strikes, I reach for my numbers: "Five!" Sometimes I even flash the other driver all five fingers, which really confuses them. I can read their lips: "What is she saying to me? Do I know this woman?" (No, thank goodness!)

Meanwhile, my kids think this is hysterical. "Boy, Mom is really having a seven kind of day!" Works like a charm. No one is offended—not the kids, not the Lord, nor anyone in earshot. Since I've more or less forgotten which number goes with what, I'm no longer dragging my mind where it doesn't want to go. And, of course, when you behave so ridiculously, you can't help but laugh at yourself.

It's not a perfect solution, but then again, I'm not a perfect woman. Just one who is aiming for the goal set before us in Proverbs: "When she speaks, her words are wise, and kindness is the rule when she gives instructions."[42]

Thank you, Lord, for the joy of numbers!
And for giving me a way to guard my tongue
and to redirect my thoughts down a more pleasing path.

SET A GOOD EXAMPLE

Let no one despise your youth, but be an example to the believers
in word, in conduct, in love, in spirit, in faith, in purity.

—1 TIMOTHY 4:12

Every seat was filled as we waited in the county clerk's office to get my driver's license renewed. Children of all ages wandered about exploring their temporary environment, as did my own two.

Lillian was a lap baby at the time (although she never stayed there), and Matthew was four and already beginning to write recognizable words. He never went anywhere without his MagnaDoodle drawing toy, and that morning was no exception.

I encouraged my sometimes-shy son to venture out to the center of the room where several kids were playing with a stack of books and games. Matthew went, dragging his MagnaDoodle behind him. A younger child was turning the pages of a colorful book, which Matthew soon became interested in too. A minute later, my son had wrestled the book out of the other child's fingers and was enjoying the brightly colored pages all by himself, leaving the little boy out of the fun.

Until that moment, I had merely watched this little drama unfold; now it was time to enter the scene. "Matthew!" I whispered sharply.

"That was not nice. Please apologize and give him back his book right away."

Looking miserable, Matthew extended the much-prized book in the tot's direction, to which the little boy responded with the toddler version of "Harrumph!" and tottered away.

Now Matthew was *really* miserable; he'd upset his mother, and some kid was unhappy with him as well. Matthew sat for a moment, staring into space while the wheels turned inside his fine young mind. Then he slowly picked up his MagnaDoodle, wrote something down, and without a word held it up for the other child to see.

The toddler ignored him, of course, because he couldn't read the words.

But I could. "I'm sorry," it said.

So simple, so profound.

Matthew couldn't bring himself to speak the words, but he could put them in writing. When the boy didn't respond as Matthew had hoped, he held up the sign again, extending it farther, with a pleading expression on his face, all to no avail.

Around the room, other mothers were beginning to notice the quiet four-year-old with wheat-colored hair and a little sign that read, "I'm sorry." I wasn't the only one who had to blink back tears. I could scarcely contain my motherly pride, until I realized that he didn't learn such humility from me.

Lord, it's clear that you were at work
in Matthew's heart that day.
Such love, faith, and purity
could only come from your example,
not mine.
But I'm willing to follow your lead Lord.
Eager, in fact.
Let me learn from my children and other little ones
what it means to set a good example.

God-Size Eyes

For the LORD does not see as man sees;
for man looks at the outward appearance,
but the LORD looks at the heart.

—1 SAMUEL 16:7B

Here's a question to kick-start your thinking this morning: What did the heroines of the Bible look like?

Let's see . . . Sarah was "a woman of beautiful countenance."[43] Yes, but what made her face so fine? Of Rebekah it was said, "The young woman was very beautiful to behold."[44] That's nice . . . but not very descriptive.

The truth is, God's Word doesn't describe the many women featured there—not by height or weight, hair color or facial features, body measurements or athletic ability.

What size dress did Ruth wear, do you suppose? Her name means "friend," but her size and shape aren't mentioned. Her exemplary character, on the other hand, is discussed at length. The woman at the well . . . a size 14, maybe? A size 10? Maybe a 22? Who knows? Who cares? The question is, What did these women *do* with their lives and how did they honor God?

I am not in any way diminishing the spiritual struggles some of us have concerning our appearance. Having worked through my own issues with self-image over many decades, I'm here to say without a doubt that the Lord cares a great deal about who we *are* and very little about what we look like.

The number of verses on these two subjects—the body and the heart—is living testimony to which one matters most to God. You'll find a half-dozen references to "sleek and fat" (but most of the time the Scripture is referring to cows!). Yet the character issues, lifestyle issues, how-you-spend-your-day issues, the stuff that really matters—these are discussed a lot more than a handful of times. God cares so much about "love," it shows up more than five hundred times. He wants us to have his "joy," and mentions it more than two hundred times. "Peace" flows like a river through the Bible hundreds of different times.

But Weight Watchers? Not in there, nor any "Lose Ten Pounds in Ten Days" schemes. Yes, fasting *is* in Scripture—not for the purpose of dieting, but for devotion. No aerobics in the wilderness, no diet aids in the desert, no rocks springing forth with Ultra Slim Fast. In fact, when you look up all those who "wasted away" in Scripture, you'll quickly discover that losing weight usually indicated *death* was right around the corner!

Even Queen Esther, whose beauty carried her to an earthly throne, spent "six months with oil of myrrh, and six months with perfumes and preparations for beautifying women."[45] But nowhere does it say, "And she did two hundred leg lifts every morning and a thousand sit-ups at night."

No, beloved. You were created by God and therefore are beautiful to him.

Rest in that.

If we measure our value by anything so temporal as the smoothness of our skin, the tightness of our tummy, or the size of our thighs, we'll be spending a great deal of money and time on something that will cease to matter once we're put in a pine box, if not sooner.

No one begins a eulogy for the dearly departed by saying, "She was so faithful to her aerobics classes, skipped desserts every chance she got, and maintained a size 8 figure throughout her marriage." I think not.

It's the example we set, the character we demonstrate, and the love we instill in others that will contribute to our sense of worth now and to our sense of contributing to future generations when we've gone on to glory.

Lord, I know you are looking at my heart,
not my outward appearance.
There are days when that thought terrifies me
because I know what's in there,
and it's not pretty.
Help me spend more time grooming my heart
according to your Word
and less time worrying about pleasing people,
who can only judge the outside me
and cannot see my heart.
But you can.

It's Never Too Late to Have a Happy Motherhood

Her children rise up and call her blessed.

—*Proverbs 31:28a*

To be blessed means to be "happy, fortunate, and to be envied."[46] My mother may have been happy and might have considered herself fortunate. But I did not envy her.

The last day I saw my mother alive was Mother's Day 1978. Four days later, she was gone, a victim of emphysema. For the next nine years, Mother's Day was the most painful day of the year for me, followed closely by every other holiday. No matter what your age, when your mother dies, part of you dies with her.

Yet, at the same time, something was also born inside me. I began to realize that motherhood, the role I had scorned through my teen years, that thankless job I never wanted, might be a pretty special task after all. My longing to be reunited with her was a constant reminder that mothers are one-of-a-kind VIPs. It was then that the desire to become a mother began to bloom in my heart.

The seeds were also planted for another harvest to come: acknowledging the sovereignty of God the Father, my heavenly parent, in a real and personal way. At Mom's funeral, I sang her favorite hymn, "Jesus Makes My Heart Rejoice," though in truth I had no heart knowledge of him at all then. It would be four more years before the words of that hymn—"I'm his sheep and know his voice"—would ring true in my heart.

So it was that my mother's death led to rebirth for me. Thank you, Mom. Again. Still. "Her children rise up"—wake up, grow up, stand up, speak up, even sing out—"and call her blessed."

Jean Fleming defines a mother as "a woman of influence. I impart values, stimulate creativity, develop compassion, modify weaknesses, and nurture strengths. I can open life up to another individual. And I can open an individual up to life."[47]

While I cannot rise up and bless my mother, I can honor her memory by giving my best effort to mothering my own children. Not by being a perfect mother, nor an always patient mother, nor a totally disciplined mother—I know my limitations! Rather, I choose to be a mother who loves God, her husband, and her children and looks for as many ways as possible to communicate to them, "I'm glad you're part of my world!"

Lord Jesus, I don't know if or when my children
will rise up and bless me.
So while I'm waiting,
I will rise up and bless you.
Bless you, bless you.
Thank you for giving me a mother
who did the best she could.

Help me do the best I can as well,
extending grace to my children
and grace to myself,
thanks to your glorious example.

Now Boarding

For as we have many members in one body,
but all the members do not have the same function,
so we, being many, are one body in Christ,
and individually members of one another.

—ROMANS 12:4–5

One of the many joys of speaking to and visiting different churches is getting a clearer understanding of the body of Christ. Two things stand out: It's big and it's different. And it's all his. No two members are exactly alike, but all members are equally important. There are no VIPs in heaven, save Jesus.

Here on earth, however, we can become members of all sorts of organizations, most of which have various levels of membership, from Prospect to Poo-bah. For example, I'm a frequent flier on several airlines, each of which has its own name for its most active customers: Priority Gold, Royal Medallion, Premier Platinum, and so forth. Bill can't keep them straight, so he tells all the gate agents, "Take care of my wife; she's a Grand Plutonium."

Sometimes we Grand Plutoniums can become a royal pain. Ask any flight attendant. On one very packed flight when every seat was filled and every passenger was grumpy, one woman in particular thought she was a little more special than everyone else. She'd gotten all settled in her aisle seat when a man kindly asked if she might switch seats with him so he could sit with his family. She gruffly refused. "This is my seat," she insisted, "and I'm a Silver Premier flier."

It seemed she would not budge.

She would live to regret this.

On our three-hour flight, the mother and daughter seated between Mrs. Silver Premier and the cabin window made at least three separate trips each to the rest room, which meant this pseudo-VIP had to put down her embroidery, fold up her service tray, and get out of her seat—not once, but half a dozen times.

I loved it.

Until a still, small voice got my attention. *Liz? There's a lesson in this. For you.*

Me? Do I act like this?

Liz, you can learn this lesson by observation . . . or by experience. Your choice.

If it's all the same to you, Lord, I'll just watch.

And learn.

We are all flying through time and space on this planet together, and we all have the opportunity to climb aboard and become members of his body. There are no special seats, no exclusive committees, no premium levels, no VIP lounges. A member is a member is a member. Different, yes, but equal.

Just as the head and hand must work together to get things done, so each part of the body of Christ contributes to our forward motion. Wise is the passenger who does her part willingly, joyfully, knowing that to be moving in his direction is enough.

Lord, you're right, as always.
More than once I've behaved exactly like
Mrs. Silver Premier—
demanding special treatment,
insisting on my way or the highway.
Help me be grateful to even
be included on the list of passengers
heading heavenward toward you.

Memory Lane

If I do not remember you,
Let my tongue cling to the roof of my mouth.

—Psalm 137:6a

I've developed a new skill: name-dropping. I don't mean slipping a few celebrity names into my conversation. I mean looking at someone I've known for ten years and not being able to remember the first letter of her first name.

"Let me introduce you to my best friend . . . my . . . er . . . uh . . . I call her *Best* for short."

For years we shunned ugly paper "Hello, My Name Is" tags with curly edges or heavy name badges that poked nasty holes in our best silk blouses. *How silly!* we'd think smugly. *Who needs name tags? I know every person at this conference, plus the names of their spouses, kids, and pet chameleon. Name badges are for old people.*

The first time your tongue gets stuck to the roof of your long-term memory, your opinion of name tags begins to shift.

Now our bifocaled eyes light up at computer-generated tags done in a big, bold font. "Hi, Joan," we confidently shout across the room. "Haven't seen you in years!"

Lately I've been wishing that all the mothers at school would embroider their names on their collars. Or wear the same clothes every time I see them, to keep the Jennys and the Judys straight. Even a big sweater with a "J" on it would help.

Actually, if I could talk the whole east end of town into permanent name tags, that would take care of my fading memory problem nicely.

Lucky for me, name tags are usually *de rigueur* at the conferences and retreats where I'm the featured speaker. People don't remember they have them on, though. I'll reach for a book to sign and say, "Is this for you, Karen?"

The color drains from her face. *How did she know?* she wonders.

I think I'm pretty clever, until I accidentally leave my own name tag on and stop by the grocery store on the way home.

"Hello, Liz Curtis Higgs!" the clerk sings out.

I smile with simpering modesty. "Oh, you read my books?"

"No, I read your name tag."

My advice? When you stumble over something you not only didn't forget but never *knew*, plead "poor memory" and start making stuff up.

Children, of course, have incredible memories. Oh, not about important items like lunch money or homework. But memorizing two thousand intricate moves on a Nintendo game? No sweat.

One of Matthew's computer games is called *Rememory.* The concept is simple: find two matching icons on a board of twenty-six different pairs. Look at two, turn them back over. Look at two more. Like *The Match Game* without the questions.

The first time through *Rememory*, my mind was a steel trap, matching icons with joy and abandon. But the second time through, my brain was a leaky tin can, still hanging on to bits and pieces of the first game. *Wasn't that green diamond-shaped thing over in this corner? What? An orange triangle? Oh, dear.* In the game of *Rememory*, I can play only once.

Bill is the serious computer geek at our house, although when I called him that once, he turned his sea-colored eyes on me and said, "That's *Dr.* Geek to you!" Watching me struggle with an unco-operative software package recently, he sighed and said, "I guess I'm going to have to break down and buy you some more memory, Liz."

If only he could.

Lord, it truly is embarrassing when I can't think of
a dear friend's name
or an important date.
Give me the grace to admit when my memory fails me,
and the compassion to forgive others
when they stare at me with a blank expression.
After so many years of living,
our brains are full, Lord.
Whisper a reminder that
such forgetfulness merely means
we're getting closer to Home.

BELIEVE IT OR NOT

Jesus said to [Martha], "I am the resurrection and the life.
He who believes in Me, though he may die, he shall live.
And whoever lives and believes in Me shall never die.
Do you believe this?"

—John 11:25–26

Do you believe, dear one? Believe that Jesus was resurrected, was raised from the dead? I had that question posed to me in the most unlikely place.

I'd been married to Bill for all of eight months and was still not pregnant. Certain I was internally broken, I sought out a new OB/GYN to see if everything was okay. *What if I can't bear children after all?* I fretted. *What if something isn't right?*

After a thorough examination, the doctor and I met in his office to discuss the results. Gently, he laughed away my concerns. "You're a perfectly healthy young woman, Liz. Why are you so worried about conceiving? It's only been eight months."

I hesitated, then began sharing a few details of my promiscuous past with him. "Doctor," I confessed, "I have this terrible fear that, with all those partners over all those years, I may have done some irreparable damage."

"Ohhh," he said, eyes wide, trying hard not to look shocked. I'd love to know what he wrote on his chart. "I, uh . . . appreciate your honesty."

"It's easy to be honest about something that's old news," I assured him, my voice becoming more confident. "I'm a Christian now, and I've been forgiven for those old sins."

"Aha!" he said suddenly, with a triumphant gleam in his eye. "If you're a Christian, can you tell me how you know, beyond a shadow of a doubt, that the Resurrection really happened, that Jesus rose from the dead?"

Boy, did that come out of left field. This must be what Paul meant when he told Timothy to be ready to preach the gospel "in season and out of season."[48] Sitting there in a little paper dress felt *very* out of season.

"Well?" The doctor leaned across his desk with expectation in his eyes.

I took a deep breath and with it came an immediate sense of peaceful assurance as the words I needed flowed from my heart and lips: "I know that Jesus is raised from the dead because he raised me from the dead. I was lost, but now I'm found. I was blind, but now I see. I was dead, but now I'm alive in Christ."

There it was. Simple, powerful, and undeniable. *Thanks, Lord.*

But the doc wasn't finished yet. "Tell me more," he insisted. So, while up and down the hall a dozen pregnant women in flimsy paper gowns waited for their obstetrician to show up, I shared with him the basic truths of the Resurrection. Namely, that Jesus is in the business of raising people from the dead. Was then, is now. Stay tuned, more to come.

Lord, help me always be prepared to give
a reason for my hope.
In any season. In any situation.
Fill me completely with the reality of you
so that anytime, anywhere,
I can respond as Martha did:
"Yes, Lord, I believe."

Spread the Word!

We loved you so much that we were delighted to share with you
not only the gospel of God but our lives as well,
because you had become so dear to us.

—*1 Thessalonians 2:8 niv*

My pastor is fond of saying that the goal of every Christian should be to "go to heaven and take as many people with you as possible."

The "go to heaven" part sounds great, but convincing people to join you sounds tricky. After all, isn't soul winning just for those believers who've officially received the spiritual gift of evangelism? (Definitely not.) What about those of us who equate leading someone to Christ with dragging a teenager up the steps to clean his or her room? (Relax, this is much easier than that.) Does every Christian woman have what it takes to share the gospel with her family and friends? (Absolutely!)

Sharing your faith simply requires caring enough about someone else to let them know how your own relationship with Christ has changed your life.

The husband-and-wife team who introduced me to Christ were brand-new believers themselves. They didn't know tons of Bible verses yet, but they knew the Savior. They hadn't memorized the

Four Spiritual Laws, but they knew how to care about people. They simply invited me into their home and welcomed me into their lives and loved me into the kingdom.

Months later, I followed their example and shared my limited but enthusiastic knowledge of the Lord with two friends at work, with the same surprising results. I wrote their names in the margin of my Bible, right next to I Thessalonians 2:8, the verse at the beginning of this chapter.

Many years and many changed lives later, I am convinced that this simple method of caring and sharing is the most effective way to "take as many people with us as possible" to heaven.

The apostle Paul wrote of "how constantly I remember you in my prayers at all times."[49] On a late evening flight to Detroit, a Northwest Airlines attendant strolled the aisle of our nearly empty plane and glanced over my shoulder at the book I was reading. "What's that about?" she asked. I grinned. It was Rebecca Pippert's classic book on lifestyle evangelism, *Out of the Saltshaker & into the World.*

I showed her the cover and said, "It's about how to share your faith."

Her eyebrows went up. "Really?"

In a casual, no-big-deal sort of way, I briefly shared my journey from a party-hearty lifestyle of drugs and promiscuity to a new life of joy and purpose in Christ.

"Really?" she said again, sitting down across the aisle from me. "It's made that much of a difference for you, huh?" At that moment, the pilot announced that we were approaching Detroit Metro

Airport. As she jumped up to resume her duties, I glanced at her name tag.

"Christine, when I get to my hotel room tonight, I'd love to remember you in prayer. Do you mind?"

Her eyes opened wide. "Would you really pray for me?"

"I'd be honored," I assured her, opening to the back cover of my book and jotting her name down.

Her teary, "Thank you!" before she headed up the aisle spoke volumes about the power of prayer, even to those who might not know the One who listens to them.

Sharing the gospel isn't so much *what* you know as *who* you know. If you know the Savior and are surrounded by friends and family who haven't met him yet, then who better to handle the introductions than you?

Lord, help me care about others enough
to share your truth with them.
Let me also give generously
of my time, energy, and resources as well.
No, more than that, Lord.
Help me give my whole life to them
and to you.
Help me neither be afraid
nor ashamed.

Putting It All in Focus

Let each of you look out not only for his own interests,
but also for the interests of others.

—PHILIPPIANS 2:4

As we near the end of our mornings together, I've noticed we're looking beyond mirrors and scales and all things *us* to see the bigger world, the world beyond our own needs. Glorious, sis.

Nothing gives you that kind of perspective like facing eternity head-on.

At a presentation I gave for cancer patients and their families, a young woman told me, "Cancer really puts life in focus for you, and prioritizing gets easy." Dauna, whose young daughter was battling cancer, offered these words of wisdom: "Every single holiday after a cancer diagnosis is more meaningful. Christmas is merrier, birthdays become more important than a national holiday, and Thanksgiving comes 365 days a year."

My presentation for those cancer patients focused on the benefits of humor for both the survivor and the supporter. They were wonderful laughers and especially appreciated the story of Gilda Radner, who fought ovarian cancer to the end by using her best weapon: humor.

When it was time for Gilda's first radiation treatment, she did all the necessary reading and brought her last three questions on three-by-five-inch cards:

1. "What are the possible side-effects?"

2. "How do I treat them?"

3. "Do you validate for parking?"[50]

Monica from Pennsylvania declared that "every bad happening has some good in it." When her husband was struck by a speeding car a few years ago, she realized that "in thirty years of marriage, Andy and I never found time to say 'I love you' to each other. We now say it 100 times a day, no matter how busy we get!"

Stories like these are a gentle reminder that the needs around us—financial, practical, emotional, or spiritual—are many. We can't meet all those needs, but we can do something. For our own sake as well as others'.

After hearing me present a program in her town, Dorothy from Iowa wrote a letter of encouragement telling me "how wonderful it was to share a happy day with you." Then she revealed a bit of her life's journey with me: When she was eight, her parents divorced; at fourteen, she had to quit school and go to work; at fifteen, she married a man "who loved me very much," and together they had six children before her husband's death at the young age of forty-nine; three of her six children suffered traumatic illnesses; she was recently diagnosed with chronic fatigue syndrome, and her seven-year-old grandson has cerebral palsy. She closed her letter, "Sending my love and prayers for your happiness."

And for yours, Dorothy. You've reminded me, and perhaps many others, of how little we have suffered on this earth compared to many. How humbling, even embarrassing, to think of the little things we've complained about, when we should be on our knees in gratitude for all that has been given to us.

> *Forgive me, Lord, for often not grasping*
> *the real definition of needy.*
> *Get my eyes off me*
> *and my focus on others.*
> *Help me find ways to lighten someone else's burden,*
> *instead of burdening others with my trivialities.*
> *You showed us how it's done, Lord.*
> *Please help me*
> *to go and do likewise.*

THE FABRIC OF
OUR LIVES

But even if I am being poured out like a drink offering
on the sacrifice and service coming from your faith,
I am glad and rejoice with all of you.

—PHILIPPIANS 2:17 NIV

Olive Schreiner said, "And it came to pass that after a time the artist was forgotten, but the work lived." As I look over my forty-plus years of living and pray for the grace of enjoying forty more, I wonder what the eighty-year-old Liz will wish she had done at forty?

I believe I can say without hesitation, I'll wish I'd been more like the role models outlined in Proverbs 31. Or simply more like one of my flesh-and-blood role models, Erma Bombeck: "When I stand before God at the end of my life, I would hope that I would have not had a single bit of talent left and could say, 'I used everything you gave me.'" Amen and amen.

Several years ago, the stage play *Quilters* came to Louisville. It's the story of a group of frontier women who traveled across America with their families, bouncing along in covered wagons, suffering every hardship known to womankind, but surviving. At every tragedy, a woman showed up at the door with a quilt in her arms, intoning, "These quilts is from the ladies of the First Baptist Church . . ."[51]

Quilts. They kept their children warm, kept the rain from coming in, and kept the wolf from their door, even when there was no door. Constructed from the scraps of their lives, they were lovingly sewn together with a thousand tiny stitches.

Quilts, like the one hanging in front of me now with "1890" carefully stitched at the bottom, made of fabrics that have lived longer than most people. Crazy quilts with no pattern at all, or intricate re-creations of the familiar old patterns—Bear Paw, Lone Star, Log Cabin, or Nine Patch.

Quilts, then and now, are legacies we leave behind for our children to cherish and, better still, to use.

When the play *Quilters* ends, the stage darkens and something called "the last unfolding" begins. The fabric-covered stage, a dull, uneven muslin, begins to lift heavenward on invisible wires. The audience gasps in surprise and delight. Before them hangs an enormous quilt, the size of the entire stage itself—huge and colorful and altogether beautiful.

The quilt pattern is, appropriately, the Tree of Life. Sarah, the matriarch, reenters the scene and delivers the final lines of the play: "Give her of the fruit of her hands, / And let her own works praise her in the gates."[52]

Oh, yes, Lord!
Such pioneer women deserve our applause
for their courage and their perseverance
despite hardships and trials.
You were with them all the way, of course.
Yet, we twenty-first-century women
have our own trails to follow
on our own deeply rutted roads.
Wrap us in the quilt of your love, Lord Jesus,
and assure us that we are not
traveling alone.

SHINE ON

The way of the righteous is like the first gleam of dawn,
which shines ever brighter until the full light of day.

—*PROVERBS 4:18* NLT

To think that we've spent a hundred mornings together (unless, of course, you nibbled on more than one slice of buttered Lizzie a day)!

It's been a delight to spend this time with you, sister mine.

Thanks for your patience as we hopped about my checkered life—different ages, different stages, different challenges. I hope a few of my own discoveries spoke to you, encouraged you, perhaps taught you something of value for your own journey.

You know what to do next and where to turn for guidance.

Jesus, who is risen, will light the way.

Shine on, beloved.

I leave my sister in your good hands, Lord.
Thank you for entrusting her heart and mind to me,
if only for two minutes each morning.
May she rise and shine
in your presence
forever.

Notes

1. Luci Swindoll, *After You've Dressed for Success* (Waco, TX: Word Books, 1987), 67.
2. Revelation 19:16
3. John 20:27
4. 1 Corinthians 9:25
5. Proverbs 23:5 NIV
6. Dr. Kevin Leman, *Bonkers* (New York: Dell Publishing, 1987), 188.
7. Proverbs 20:29 NIV
8. Matthew 21:22
9. John 15:26
10. Genesis 1:3
11. Isaiah 40:8b
12. Ephesians 5:22
13. Ephesians 5:25
14. Revelation 19:13
15. W. Vine, *Vine's Expository Dictionary of the Bible,* vol. 4 (Old Tappan, NJ: Fleming H. Revell Company, 1981), 230.
16. Psalm 90:2b
17. John 19:30
18. Acts 27:34
19. See Matthew 5:48.

20. Philippians 1:6

21. Song of Solomon 8:6

22. LaJoyce Martin, *Mother Eve's Garden Club* (Sisters, OR: Multnomah Books, 1993), 157.

23. Jill Briscoe, *Queen of Hearts* (Old Tappan, NJ: Fleming H. Revell Company, 1984), 9.

24. Frank E. Gaeblein, *The Expositor's Bible Commentary,* vol. 5 (Grand Rapids, MI: Zondervan Publishing House, 1991), 1128.

25. Matthew 18:4

26. Annie Chapman with Maureen Rank, *Smart Women Keep It Simple* (Minneapolis: Bethany House Publishing, 1992), 15.

27. Anthony Campolo Jr., *The Success Fantasy* (Wheaton, IL: Victor Books, 1980), 109.

28. Proverbs 23:20–21

29. Matthew 6:33

30. Ecclesiastes 3:15a

31. John 14:27a

32. Colossians 3:15

33. 1 Corinthians 15:45

34. Job 18:9 NIV

35. Matthew 7:28–29

36. Matthew 6:11 NIV

37. Ecclesiastes 3:1

38. Proverbs 31:11 NIV

39. Elizabeth Cody Newenhuyse, *The Woman with Two Heads* (Waco, TX: Word Books, 1991), 51–52.

40. See Proverbs 31:12 AMP.

41. Hebrews 13:8
42. Proverbs 31:26 NLT
43. Genesis 12:11
44. Genesis 24:16
45. Esther 2:12
46. Proverbs 31:28 AMP
47. Jean Fleming, *A Mother's Heart* (Colorado Springs, CO: NavPress, 1982), 27.
48. 2 Timothy 4:2
49. Romans 1:9-10 NIV
50. Gilda Radner, *It's Always Something* (New York: Avon, 1990), 205.
51. Molly Newman and Barbara Damashek, *Quilters* (New York: Dramatists Play Service, Inc., 1986), 52.
52. Proverbs 31:31

ALSO BY LIZ CURTIS HIGGS

∽

Books, Workbooks, and Videos
Bad Girls of the Bible
Really Bad Girls of the Bible
Unveiling Mary Magdalene

∽

Historical Fiction
Thorn in My Heart
Fair Is the Rose

∽

Contemporary Fiction
Mixed Signals
Bookends

∽

Children's Books
The Pumpkin Patch Parable
The Parable of the Lily
The Sunflower Parable
The Pine Tree Parable
Go Away, Dark Night

ABOUT THE AUTHOR

A native of Lancaster County, Pennsylvania, Liz Curtis Higgs spent ten years as a popular radio personality in Pennsylvania, Maryland, Indiana, Michigan, and Kentucky, before she discovered the thrill of speaking before a live audience: AN ENCOURAGER® was born. Since becoming a professional speaker in 1986, Liz has presented more than fifteen hundred encouraging programs for audiences in all fifty states and around the globe.

The author of numerous adult and children's books, Liz is also the editor of an annual newsletter, *The Graceful Heart,* and is a columnist for *Today's Christian Woman* magazine with her back-page feature, "Life with Liz." Feature articles about Liz have appeared in newspapers and magazines across the country, and she has been interviewed on more than six hundred radio and television stations.

Liz and her husband, Bill, have two children, Matthew and Lillian, and one old house on Laughing Heart Farm.

If you would like more information on Liz's free newsletter or her books, videos, and presentations, please visit her Web site—***www.LizCurtisHiggs.com***—or contact her at:

Liz Curtis Higgs
P.O. Box 43577
Louisville, KY 40253-0577